100개의 브로치

100 BROOCHES

목차
Contents

백인백색의 만화경

브로치로 본 한국의 현대장신구

전용일

장신구를 감상하는 일은 마치 만화경을 보는 것과 같다. 장신구에 담긴 형태와
재질, 그들의 이미지와 서사를 살피고 공감하는 일은, 작은 원통의 만화경 속에서
거울 벽면들 사이로 펼쳐지는 색색의 유리와 종이조각들이 만드는 예측불허한
패턴을, 그 환상의 세계를 좇는 것과 닮았다. 특별히 작가의 창의적 발상이 담긴
장신구라면, 감상자는 만화경의 입구에 눈을 바짝 대고 천천히 통을 돌리며
그 작은 집 속에서 펼쳐지는 시각의 파노라마를 읽어내는 집중력이 필요할
것이다. 이는 작은 미술로서의 장신구가 갖는 특징이면서, 아직도 일반인들에게는
낯선 현대장신구를 이해하기 위해서, 작가들의 수고만큼이나 보는 이들의 노력과
경험이 필요하다는 의미이기도 하다.

전통과 이탈의 길항작용

오랜 역사 속에서 장신구 작가는 다음의 두 가지 재능을 지닌 이들이었다. 첫째는
귀한 재료를 다루고 완벽히 통제하는 장인적 기술이다. 그것은 세상에서 가장
단단하고 다루기 어려운 재료인 금속, 특히 금과 은이라는 귀금속을 가공하는
능력이다. 이에 더해 보석과 같은 희귀재를 가공해 금속의 구조 속에 안전하게
고정함으로써, 착용하거나, 휴대하거나, 보관하기 편리한 형태로 만드는 세공
능력을 뜻한다. 두 번째 재능은 앞의 기술을 발휘해 형태를 구현하는 과정에서
발휘되는 시각적 통제력 혹은 심미안이라고 할 수 있다. 시대와 지역에 따라 다른
미적 기준에도 불구하고, 장신구의 시각적 밀도를 높이고 화려함을 더함으로써
관람자의 시선을 끌어당기는 능력이다. 오랜 숙련과 경험으로 체득하는
제작자의 두 가지 능력은 장신구를 작지만 밀도가 높은 시각적인 결정체로,
재화의 일종으로, 그리고 착용자 개인이나 그 사회가 나누는 각종 의미를 전하는

기표로서 세상에 제공해 왔다.

이러한 전통은 20세기 후반 새로운 장신구의 등장과 함께 변화를 맞는다. 유럽과
미국에서 일군의 작가들은 장신구를 일종의 창작과 발언의 미술적 매체로 여겨,
표현내용을 우선하기 시작했다. 1960년대 현대장신구의 등장은 전통의 단절이나
대체라기보다 기존의 장신구와 병행하는 새로운 선택지의 등장이라는 표현이
적합할 것 같다. 새로운 조류는 전통적 장신구, 혹은 금속공예 분야와 많은 부분을
공유하고 있음에도 불구하고 여러 측면에서 급격한 변화를 만들었다. 신체성,
장식성, 재화적 가치, 사회적 상징성 등 장신구의 전통적 형식과 가치는 필수가
아닌 선택이 되었으며, 작가들은 개인적이거나 사회적인 이슈, 혹은 장신구
형식과 한계에 대한 모색 등의 개념적 내용을 주제로 다뤘고, 방법적으로는
금속에서 벗어나 거의 모든 종류의 재료를 장신구에 도입하는 획기적인 변화를
만들었다. 지난 50년 동안의 현대장신구의 궤적은 장신구 본연의 정체성과 미학적
확장이라는 두 가지 지향점을 오가며 상호 영향을 준 변증법적 과정이라고 할 수
있다. 이러한 변화를 우리는 수많은 동시대 작가의 현대장신구 작품을 통해 살펴볼
수 있는데, 특히 이들 작품 목록의 다수가 브로치라는 것부터 매우 흥미롭다.

브로치, 현대장신구의 창틀

브로치가 현대장신구의 대표적 품목이 된 데에는 몇 가지 이유가 있다. 우선,
인체의 전면 상부에서 드러나는 브로치는 관람자에게 주목의 대상이 된다.
각종 메시지나 구호가 담긴 배지, 국가적 보훈의 표상인 훈장이 브로치와 같은
형식으로 제작되어 착용된다는 점도 이 주목성에 기인한다. 브로치의 원형은
고대 로마 시대부터 상용했던, 주로 의상을 고정하거나 여미기 위한 핀의 일종인
피블라fibula로, 그 기원은 청동기시대까지 소급된다. 피블라는 시간이 흐르며 점차
옷을 위한 실용적 기능에서 벗어나 장식적, 상징적 기능이 강조되면서 브로치의
원형이 되었다. 중세에 이미 보석 등으로 치장된 고가의 장식물로서 브로치가
제작되어 세공가의 역량이 집결되는 몸 위의 예술품으로 자리 잡았으며, 이후
각 시대의 스타일과 상징성을 전하는 장신구의 대표적 품목이 되어 우리
시대에까지 전해졌다.

브로치는 다른 점에서도 유리하다. 재료에 따라 크기에서도 비교적 자유로우며,
신체 위에 놓여야 하는 평면적^{부조적} 조건에도 불구하고 다양한 입체적, 공간적
구조가 가능하다. 목이나 팔목, 손가락을 감는 목걸이, 팔찌, 반지처럼 루프 형이 될

필요도 없으며, 별도의 잠금장치가 필요하지도 않다. 의상에 고정하기 위해 뒷면에 부착하는 핀pin-back을 제외하면, 독립적인 입체물, 즉 오브제에 가깝다. 자유로운 형태적 실험과 표현을 원하는 현대장신구 작가에게 브로치가 효과적인 매체인 이유이다. 장신구를 걸어 다니는 조각이라고 표현할 때 이에 가장 걸맞은 품목 역시 브로치라고 할 수 있다. 때론 인체와의 관계, 장식성, 착용성을 응용한 주제를 통해, 때론 인체로부터 이탈하는 일종의 오브제로서, 브로치는 현대장신구의 다면적인 모습을 보여주는 창이 된다. 200점의 브로치를 통해 한국 현대장신구의 흐름과 다양한 스타일을 일람하는 두 차례의 브로치 기획전은 브로치의 위와 같은 특징에 기반하고 있다.

100인 작가들의 목록

2020년의 「100개의 브로치 ― 한국 현대장신구의 새로운 세대」 전시는 50인의 작가가 만든 100점의 브로치를 통해 한국 현대장신구의 다양성을 보여주고 역사적 의미를 기록하려는 의도로 개최되었다.[1] 기획자 이동춘은 전시회를 통해 개별 작가들의 작품을 소개함과 동시에, 세 개의 시기 구분으로 한국 현대장신구의 시대적 변화를 추적했다. 1980년대 금속공예의 하위장르로 시작되고 해외 유학파 작가의 영향이 강했던 **시작기**, 1990년대 말 등장한 초기 전업 장신구작가들의 활동기인 **전문화기**, 그리고 2000년대 중반 이후 등장한 다수의 현대장신구 작가들이 국내외에서 활발하게 활동한 시기인 **확장기**이다.

첫 전시로부터 4년이 지난 2024년 올해, 후속의 기획전 「100개의 브로치 ― 한국 현대장신구의 새로운 세대」를 개최해, 젊은 세대를 중심으로 다시 선정한 50명 작가의 작품 100점을 전시한다. 1차 기획의 결과물에 미래적 가능성의 모색을 추가함으로써, 두 차례의 프로젝트는 결과적으로 100인의 한국 현대장신구 작가의 목록과 연대기를 완성했다. 작가 1인당 브로치 2점으로 제한된 조건은 한국의 현대장신구의 전모를 파악하기에 부족하다고 할 수 있다. 그러나 한편으로, 같은 품목을 다루는 작가의 서로 다른 발상과 스타일의 변화 등을 한눈에 살필 수 있는 파노라믹 뷰를 제공해준다는 점에서 흥미롭다.

100인의 작가 목록을 통해 우리는 한국 현대장신구의 몇 가지 단면을 엿볼 수 있다. 우선, 나이를 분류해 보면, 70대 4명, 60대 6명, 50대 19명, 40대 41명, 30대 26명 20대 4명으로 전체 작가의 67%가 30대와

1
전용일, '장식과 탐미의 변증법 ― 한국의 현대장신구 이야기', ‹100개의 브로치 ― 한국 현대장신구의 새로운 세대›, 소금나무, 2020, 첫 번째 기획전의 서문인 이 글을 통해 한국에서의 현대장신구의 성립배경과 전개과정, 그리고 현황 등을 개괄적으로 작성했다.

40대에 속해 있음을 알 수 있다. 평균 25세에 작가 활동을 개시했다고 전제할 때, 40대 작가는 2000년 이후, 20, 30대 작가의 경우에는 2010년 이후 작가의 이력을 시작했다고 볼 수 있다. 이로써 미술계 전체는 물론, 공예 분야 내에서도 현대장신구는 매우 젊은 분야이며 그 역사가 매우 짧다는 사실을 알 수 있다.

작가들의 교육적 배경을 통해서도 한국 현대장신구의 특징이 드러난다. 현대장신구의 태동은 미술대학 교육과 불가분의 관계에 있다. 1960년대 현대장신구를 주도한 유럽의 작가들이 그렇듯이, 한국의 현대장신구 역시 그 시작을 미술대학 출신의 작가가 이끌었다. 이번 참여작가 100인 경우에도 대학에서 금속공예 혹은 장신구를 수학하지 않은 경우는 한 명도 없다. 개인 작가 혹은 공방을 통한 도제교육이나 독학에 의한 작가적 수련은 불가능한 걸까, 장신구 제작이 대학이라는 교육체계 안에 있어야 하는 이유는 무엇일까, 하는 질문들이 떠오른다. 향후 현대장신구의 다양성과 관련해서 생각해 볼 만한 문제이다.

작가들의 해외 유학의 비중이 매우 높은 점도 특기할 만하다. 공예 분야 중에서도 유독 금속공예와 장신구는 초기부터 해외 유학파가 많았으며, 그 결과 많은 부분에서 서구의 교육체계와 내용이 이식되고 그 영향력이 지속되었다. 초기의 유학지는 주로 미국이었으며, 이후에는 독일과 기타 유럽국가들, 혹은 일본 등으로 다양해졌다. 100인의 작가 중 해외 유학을 경험한 이는 42명이며, 국가별로는 미국 18명, 독일 15명, 영국 4명, 프랑스 2명, 이탈리아 2명, 그리고 일본, 스웨덴, 캐나다, 벨기에, 핀란드가 각 1명이다. 발생 초기부터 유학의 비중이 높았던 이유는, 다른 분야에 비해 교육적 기반이 취약했던 현대 금속공예와 장신구 분야에 해외의 선진적 교육이 필요했다는 점, 그리고 학력 중에서도 특히 유학 경력이 높이 평가받은 한국의 사회적 인식이 오랜 기간 작동한 점을 들 수 있다. 그러나 2010년대 이후 두 가지 측면 모두에 큰 변화가 생겼다. 공예 교육의 질에서 결코 서구가 우리보다 앞섰다고 볼 수 없으며, 유학 경력을 높이 평가하는 사회적 통념 역시 오늘에 이르러 희박해졌는데, 국내 교육을 통해서 작품의 질적 수준과 동시대적 스타일을 담보하고 공유할 수 있게 되었다는 의미이기도 하다.

다양성과 공통점

두 차례의 기획을 통해 전시되는 200점의 작품은 브로치라는 형식적 유사성에도 불구하고 매우 다양한 방식으로 드러난다. 형태, 공간, 재질 등 일차적 외관이 각양각색이며, 이들이 표현하는 이미지와 주제도 매우 다양하다. 마치 프리즘의

분광처럼 폭넓은 스펙트럼을 만들고 있어 **백인백색**이라는 말이 결코 지나치지 않다.

다양성을 살펴보는 것에 비해 이들을 유형화하거나 시대별 특징을 찾아내는 일은
쉽지 않다. **시작, 전문화, 확장, 새로운 세대**라는 시대적 구분은 비교적 유효하지만,
각 시기를 모두 합쳐도 40년밖에 되지 않으며, 2024년 현재의 시점에서도 거의
모든 작가가 현역으로 활동하며 상호 영향을 주고받기 때문이다. 재료에 따른
분류는 가능하나 작품에서 차지하는 재료의 비중이 작가마다 달라 기준으로 삼기
어렵다. 젊은 작가의 경우, 빈번한 해외 교류와 신기술의 활용 등 외부적 영향에
의한 변화가 계속되고 있어 더욱 틀에 넣기 어렵다. 이와 같은 사항들을 고려한다면
작품의 분류나 유형화보다 전체의 작품들을 통해 나타나는 한국의 현대장신구가
보여주는 몇 가지 특징을 도출해보는 것이 더 타당할 듯하다.

첫째, 한국 작가들의 작품은 대체로 기술적으로 뛰어나다. 작품의 완성도가 높으며,
기술적 우위로 인해 세부의 표현이 다양하고 섬세하다. 섬세한 세부는 장식적이며
직관적인 볼거리를 제공한다. 교육과정에서 손 도구를 활용하는 수공 기술이
강조되며, 상대적으로 기계의 활용에는 어두운 편이다. 숙련된 손기술은 재료를
장악하는 힘이라는 점에서 전통적인 금속재는 물론 현대장신구가 추구하는 다양한
재료의 도입과 활용에도 유리하다. 둘째, 한국의 현대장신구에서 재료가 차지하는
비중이 매우 높다. 한국의 작가들에게 재료는 소재이면서 동시에 주제인 경우가
많다. 재료의 물성이 작품의 가장 중요한 특징이 되는 경우가 많으며, 재료가
작가의 정체성을 만들어 지속되는 경우도 많다. 이 경향은 2000년대 중반 금속에서
비금속으로 재료가 확장되면서 더욱 심화하였다. 결과적으로 한국의 현대장신구는
사변적이라기보다 물질적이고 직관적이며, 기호성보다 즉물성이 두드러진다.
셋째, 형태적 다양성에도 불구하고 여전히 많은 한국 작가들은 유기적이며
비정형적인 추상 형태를 다룬다. 이 경향은 자연물이나 인체로부터 추출한 추상
형태를 통해 서정적 이미지를 추구한 앞선 세대일수록 뚜렷하다. 2000년대 이후
유럽 공예의 영향이 강해지고 국제적 교류가 빈번해지면서 형태적 언어 역시
다양해졌으나, 물성의 탐구를 중점적으로 다루는 작가들이 포진한 한국의 경우,
유기적 형태가 여전히 우세하다고 말할 수 있다.

연대기적 비전
요약한다면, 한국의 현대장신구 작가들은 기술적 수월성을 바탕으로, 재료로부터
아이디어를 얻는 경향이 많으며, 재질을 강조하는 유기적, 비정형적 추상 형태를

선호한다. 이와 같은 특징은 강점이자 약점이다. 우리 시대가 강조하는 창의성 혹은 개념성의 기준에서 본다면, 기술과 물성에 대한 의존은 일종의 한계가 될 수 있다. 반면에 잘 만들어진 오브제로서 강렬한 시각적 이미지를 드러내는 덕분에, 별도의 설명 없이도 폭넓은 관객에게 직관적으로 다가가는 장점을 지녔다고 할 수 있다. 최근 10년 이상 한국의 현대장신구가 유럽을 비롯해 국제무대에서 환영받고 있는 것은 이러한 특징들이 약점보다는 강점으로 발휘된 것이라고 할 수 있다.

두 차례의 기획전이 선보이는 200점의 브로치는 한국의 현대장신구를 한눈에 훑어볼 수 있는 전망 좋은 창이다. 4년 전의 1차 기획을 통해 현대장신구의 성립과 전개 과정이라는 과거를 조감할 수 있었다면, 올해의 2차 기획에서는 젊은 작가들을 중심으로 한 현재진행형의 다양한 현상과 미래적 가능성을 가늠할 수 있다. 첫 번째 기획전으로 앞선 세대의 작가들이 역사에 포함된 자신의 성취를 확인할 수 있었다면, 이번에는 연대기의 연장선에서 젊은 세대가 새로운 도전을 다짐하는 시작점이 될 것이다.

성취와 도전은 이 분야의 활동을 새롭게 바라보아야 하는 미래의 과제로 이어진다. 그것은 지금까지와는 다른, 새로운 논의일지도 모른다. 거기에는 장신구, 혹은 현대장신구라는 울타리 속에서 안주하던 시각적, 미학적 의미를 넘어서 사회적, 경제적, 대중적 차원의 의미를 성찰하는 일이 포함되어야 할 것이다.[2] 이는 한국의 현대장신구가 다음 세대로 이어지는 지속 가능한 활동이 되기 위한 조건이다. 두 차례의 기획전이 의도한 연대기는, 서사의 마지막 부분에 위치한 미래에 어떤 종류의 비전과 과제를 담을 것인가를 생각하는 일로 다시 시작된다.

전용일은 금속공예가, 교육자로 활동하며 여러 매체에 공예 관련의 글을 기고했다. 저서 「금속공예기법」, 「디자인공예대사전(공저)」이 있으며, 2020년의 「100개의 브로치-한국현대장신구연대기」 기획전의 서문을 통해 한국 현대장신구의 성립 배경과 전개에 관한 글을 썼다.

2
전용일, 앞의 글. 2020. 이 글에서 한국의 현대장신구가 가진 문제와
한계에 관해서 비교적 상세히 언급했으므로 여기서는 생략한다.

A Kaleidoscope of 100 Distinctive Artists
Exploring Korean Contemporary Jewelry through Brooches

Yong-il Jeon

Jewelry offers the viewer an experience similar to looking through a kaleidoscope. When observing and identifying with the shape, material, image, and narrative embodied in jewelry, the viewer is drawn into a fantasy world that resembles the unforeseeable patterns formed by colorful pieces of glass and paper in between the mirrors of a small cylinder kaleidoscope. To fully appreciate the artist's creative idea behind jewelry, it is required to have a certain level of concentration that is equivalent to carefully placing one's eye on the hole of a kaleidoscope and slowly rotating the tube to capture the visual panorama unfold in a tiny container. Therefore, in order to understand contemporary jewelry, which is still unfamiliar to the general public, the viewer needs appreciate it as a small art piece and put in the amount of effort and experience devoted by the artist while making it.

The Antagonism between Tradition and Divergence
Throughout its long history, jewelry artists have shown that they have two qualities. One is the craftsmanship to handle and perfectly control precious materials. It is an ability to process metals, especially precious metals such as gold and silver, which are the most solid and difficult materials to handle. Moreover, it also refers to the skills of processing rare materials such as gems and setting them in a metal structure to make it wearable, portable, or storable. The other one is the visual control or aesthetic sense conveyed in the process of creating a form using the previously mentioned crafting skills. A jewelry artist can increase the level of visual density and extravagance to captivate people regardless of how different aesthetic standards are depending on the era and region. Based on these two qualities, which are acquired through a long period of training and experience, jewelry makers can create a multi-purposed small but dense visual object, which can serve as a commodity, as well as an indicator that carries all sorts of meanings shared by an individual wearer or society.

In the late 20th century, the emergence of a new jewelry scene changed the traditional features of jewelry. As a group of artists in Europe and the United States began to approach jewelry as an artistic medium that communicates the artist's creativity and voice, the focus of jewelry artists shifted to crafting details of expressions. The inception of contemporary jewelry in the 1960s was when a new alternative that is equivalent, rather than breaking from or replacing, to traditional jewelry surfaced. This new trend has brought notable changes in many ways, despite its similarities with traditional jewelry, or metalworks. Traditional forms and values of jewelry such as physical and decorative features, commodity value, social symbolism and others, have become matters of choice as artists began to employ innovative changes. For example, artists began to not only use conceptual ideas as subjects, such as personal or social issues, and their studies on jewelry forms and its limits, but also consider any materials possible that are non-metallic. Contemporary jewelry have been caught in a dialectical cycle over the last 50 years, shifting back and forth between the true identity of jewelry and its aesthetic extension, eventually influencing both ends. These changes are evident in numerous pieces of jewelry created by contemporary artists and it is especially interesting that most of their works are brooches.

The Brooch, A Window into Contemporary Jewelry

There are a few reasons the brooch has become an exemplar of contemporary jewelry. Firstly, a brooch is typically worn on the upper front of the body making it the subject of attention. Similar examples that are made and worn to attract attention are badges, which carry various messages or slogans, as well as medals for national patriotism. The archetype of brooches is a type of pin used to fix or fasten clothes known as fibula, which can be traced back to the bronze age. The fibula gradually served as a prototype for the brooch over time, during which its decorative and symbolic features were highlighted, rather than its practical functions. In medieval times, the brooch was not only made as an expensive accessory decorated with gem stones, but also perceived as an artwork of the craftsman's techniques displayed on the body. Afterwards, the brooch became a classical type of jewelry that represents the style and symbolism of each generation, which continues till this day.

Brooches are favored in other aspects as well. In terms of size and shape, brooches are relatively free from size limitations depending on the material, and can be designed into various three-dimensional and spatial structures, despite the conditions of the human body, which has a flat relief surface. Moreover, brooches do not require a specific design for it to be worn like loop-shaped necklaces and bracelets, or rings, nor is it necessary to have a separate fastening device. However, a brooch needs a pin-back to be attached on the back in order to be fixed on clothes, other than that, it is equivalent to a freestanding three-dimensional structure, in other words, an object. That is why the brooch is considered as an effective medium for artists, who prefer to have freedom in experimenting with form and expressing themselves. Jewelry is normally referred to as a walking sculpture and the brooch can be seen as the most qualified type of jewelry that lives up to that expression. The brooch serves as a window to various aspects of contemporary jewelry not only with its subject, which draws upon relationships with the human body, decorative potentials, and wearability, but also as a certain type of object that is autonomous from the body. Two exhibitions, which compiled the trends and various styles of Korean contemporary jewelry through 200 pieces of brooches, are based on the features mentioned above.

The List of 100 Artists

The 2020 exhibition, 「100 Brooches—Korean Contemporary Jewelry Chronicle」 aimed to present the diversity of Korean contemporary jewelry and document its historical significance through 100 pieces of brooches created by 50 artists.[1] Through this exhibition, the curator, Dongchun Lee introduced the works of these artists, as well as categorized the history of Korean contemporary jewelry into three time periods and traced how it changed across time. The 1980s can be defined as the **foundation** phase when contemporary jewelry started out as a sub-genre of metalworking and artists who have studied abroad had a strong influence over the practice; the late 1990s was a period of **specialization** as full-time jewelry artists emerged during this time; after the mid-2000s contemporary jewelry began its **expansion** stage since many artists became active in Korea and abroad.

The exhibition, 「100 Brooches—A New Generation of Korean Contemporary Jewelry」 opens in 2024, which marks the fourth year since the first exhibition in 2020. For this exhibition, 50 artists were mainly selected among the new generation of artists to present 100 brooches. Moreover, this year's exhibition complements the previous exhibition and completes the list and chronicle of 100 Korean contemporary jewelry artists by exploring the future potential of the genre. In addition, by limiting the number of brooches exhibited by each artist to two pieces may have given us an incomplete picture of Korean contemporary jewelry and narrowed our understanding, however, it is interesting to see how limiting the number of pieces per artist results in a panoramic view over the different approaches and changes in the styles

1
Yong-il Jeon, 'The Dialectic of ornament and aesthetic-the story of Korean contemporary jewelry', ‹100 Brooches-Korean Contemporary Jewelry Chronicle›, Salt Tree, 2020. As the preface for the first exhibition, it introduces the background and development of contemporary jewelry in Korea and its current status.

applied to the same type of jewelry.

The list of 100 artists sheds light on certain aspects of Korean contemporary jewelry. First of all, the list reveals the number of artists by age group: 4 in their 70s, 6 in their 60s, 19 in their 50s, 41 in their 40s, 26 in their 30s, and 4 in their 20s. Thus, 67% of the artists are in their 30s and 40s. Assuming that the average age at which an artist begins one's career is 25, then artists in their 40s may have begun after 2000, while those in their 20s or 30s would have begun after 2010. Based on the data, it can be concluded that contemporary jewelry is a very young field not only within the entire art domain, but also within the field of crafts.

Moreover, certain characteristics of Korean contemporary jewelry can be defined according to the educational backgrounds of the artists. The beginning of contemporary jewelry is closely acquainted with the inclusion of art at a higher education level. Korean artists who studied at art universities paved the way for contemporary jewelry, which is similar to the case of European artists who led the sector in the 1960s. Every single one of the 100 artists who participated in the two exhibitions studied either metal craft or jewelry at a higher education institute. Some questions come to mind such as "Is it impossible to become an artist through apprenticeships at studios or a self-taught artist?", "What is the reason to have jewelry production taught at higher education institutions?" These are some issues that should be taken into consideration to ensure a certain level of diversity within the field of contemporary jewelry in the future.

Furthermore, it is noteworthy that the ratio of artists who have studied abroad to those who haven't is very high. Especially, there were more artists from metalworking and jewelry who went overseas to study in the early days compared to other sectors in the crafts, thus the field has been highly influenced by the Western education system and materials. In the beginning, a majority of artists chose to study in the United States, however, later on artists began to seek alternative places to study, such as Germany and other European countries, as well as Japan. Among the 100 artists, 42 have studied abroad: 18 in the United States, 15 in Germany, 4 in the United Kingdom, 2 in France, 2 in Italy, and the remaining 5 each studied in Japan, Sweden, Canada, Belgium, and Finland. The majority of contemporary metalwork and jewelry artists have chosen to study abroad in the early days to receive advanced education since the educational foundation for contemporary jewelry in Korea was weak compared to other sectors. Moreover, there was a long-standing social perception of thinking highly of those with overseas academic experience. However, after the 2010s, there was a major shift in both aspects. There has been a consensus that it is difficult to determine that the West is more advanced than Korea in terms of the quality of craft education, whereas the social convention of valuing the experience of studying abroad has become insubstantial, which also means that it became possible to secure and share the quality and contemporary style of craft art within the domestic education system.

Diversity and Similarities

The 200 brooches from the both exhibitions present various approaches taken by artists, despite the similarities in terms of form. For example, the brooches display a diverse range of primary external features such as shape, space, and material, as well as the images and subjects they represent. Therefore, the exhibition title, **100 Distinctive Artists** is not an exaggeration as the exhibited brooches form a wide spectrum resembling a dispersive prism.

Although defining stages such as **foundation**, **specialization**, **expansion**, and **new generation**, may seem relatively relevant in comparison to classifying the diverse range of contemporary jewelry, it is difficult to group the works or link each characteristic to a specific era due to its short history of 40 years and the fact that currently in 2024, almost all of the participating artists are still active and have interactions with one another. Even though categorizing the brooches by material is possible, it is difficult to set a standard since the proportion of the materials in each piece is different depending on the artist. In the case of young artists, who are constantly influenced by external factors, such as frequent foreign exchanges and the use of new technology, it is even more challenging to confine them in a particular group. Therefore, it is reasonable to define a few characteristics that represent Korean contemporary jewelry based on all of the works, rather than focusing on classifying or categorizing them.

First of all, Korean artists are overall excellent in terms of technique. The level of execution on their works is up to perfection, whereas the various and exquisite details that are crafted with superior technical skills are both decorative and intuitively appealing. These artists have received an education that is relatively focused on handicraft skills using tools compared to handling machines. Especially, artists with exceptional handicraft techniques have control over materials, which allows them to choose various types of materials preferred in contemporary jewelry, as well as traditional metallic materials.

Secondly, material plays a dominant role in Korean contemporary jewelry. For Korean artists, materials are not only used as a resource, but also considered as subjects. For instance, there are many works in which materiality is the most prominent feature, thus building a consistent identity for the artist. This trend was at its peak during the mid-2000s, when artists began to use non-metallic materials. As a result, Korean contemporary jewelry can be characterized as materialistic and intuitive, rather than conceptual, as it displays physical qualities that are more dominating than its symbolic features.

Lastly, there are still many Korean artists who create organic abstract forms, despite its morphological diversity. This is evident in previous generations that pursued lyrical images through abstract shapes that are derived from natural objects or the human body. After the 2000s, languages of form has become increasingly diverse, due to the rising influence of European craft and international exchanges, however in Korea, a majority of artists still prefer organic forms as they tend to mainly focus on exploring materiality in their work.

Chronological Vision

In sum, Korean contemporary jewelry artists, who have excellent technical skills, tend to capture ideas from their choice of material, and prefer to create organic abstract forms that can highlight the qualities of the material. These features can work both as an advantage or disadvantage to an artist. On one hand, the dependence on techniques and materiality can limit the artist in terms of creativity or conceptuality, which are considered as important traits in jewelry today. On the other hand, artists, who create powerful visual images of well-made objects can intuitively approach a wider audience without having the need to explain themselves. In the end, these features have had a positive impact than a negative one on Korean contemporary jewelry, as Korean artists have been welcomed to the international scene, including Europe, for more than a decade.

The 200 brooches presented over two exhibitions are an excellent gateway to overview Korean contemporary jewelry. The first exhibition, which was held four years ago, provided an extensive perspective on the establishment of contemporary jewelry and its development, whereas the second exhibition held this year presents various ongoing trends led by young artists and future potentials. If the first exhibition provided the artists from the previous generation an opportunity to see how their achievements made a mark in history, then the second exhibition will serve as a stepping stone for the younger generation to fully commit themselves to taking on new challenges and continuing this narrative.

These accomplishments and challenges leave us with a future mission to approach contemporary jewelry from a new standpoint. This may become a new matter of debate different from before, including reflections from a social, economic, and public perspective that are beyond the visual and aesthetic issues grounded in the field of jewelry or contemporary jewelry. [2] This is essential for Korean contemporary jewelry to become a sustainable practice that continues for generations. At the end of this chronology, which is based on these two exhibitions, we will be taken back to the starting point to face questions about what kind of vision and challenges will exist in the future.

Yong-il Jeon is a metalsmith and educator, Jeon has contributed writings about crafts to various media titles. Books written by Jeon include 「Techniques of Metalsmithing and Jewelry Making」, 「Encyclopedia of Design & Craft (coauthor)」, and he also wrote about the background of how Korean contemporary jewelry was pioneered and developed in the preface for the 2020 exhibition, 「100 Brooches–Korean Contemporary Jewelry Chronicle」.

2
Yong-il Jeon, previous reference. 2020. The issues and limitations of Korean contemporary jewelry have been written in detail in the 2020 preface, thus it will not be covered in this publication.

브로치

BROOCHES

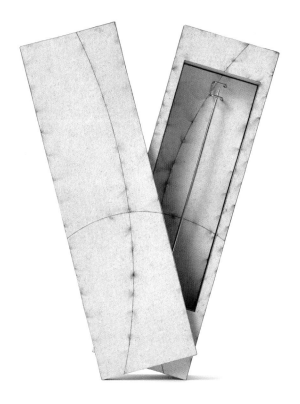

김경진 Kyungjin Kim

지금 이 순간 #1 This moment #1 하드보드지, 자석, 황동, 와이어 hardboard, magnet, brass, wire   3×10×3cm   2024

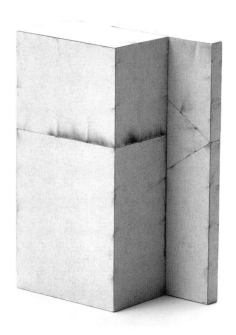

지금 이 순간 #2 This moment #2   하드보드지, 자석, 와이어 hardboard, magnet, wire   4×8×3cm   2024

이영주 Youngjoo Lee

산들바람 2024_b01 A gentle breeze 2024_b01   스테인리스 스틸, 분체도장 stainless steel, powder coating   9×8×4.5cm   2024

산들바람 2024_b02 A gentle breeze 2024_b02   스테인리스 스틸, 분체도장 stainless steel, powder coating   10×10×6cm   2024

한주희 Joohee Han

타나토스 I Thanatos I   계란껍데기, 하드폼, 석고, 안료, 황동 eggshell, hard foam, plaster, pigment, brass   9×11×7cm   2024

타나토스 II Thanatos II 계란껍데기, 하드폼,
석고, 안료, 황동 eggshell, hard foam,
plaster, pigment, brass 10×11×7cm 2024

강미나 Mina Kang

잔상 1 Afterimage 1 모시, 실, 정은, 스테인리스 스틸 ramie fabric, thread, sterling silver, stainless steel 8×8.5×5cm 2024

잔상 2 Afterimage 2   모시, 실, 정은, 스테인리스 스틸 ramie fabric, thread, sterling silver, stainless steel   10×10×5cm   2024

김수진 Sujin Kim

그 순간/바다 The Moment/Sea   자수, 월넛, 백동, 정은, 스프레이 페인트 embroidery, walnut wood, nickel silver, sterling silver, spray paint
4.6×7.5×2.8cm   2024

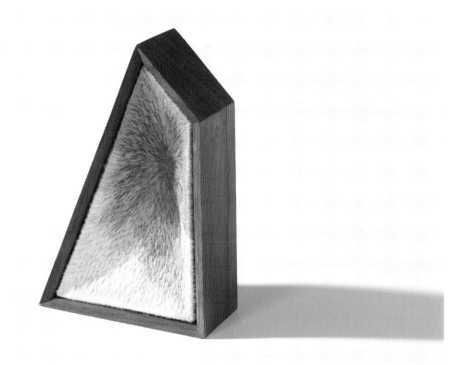

그 순간/노을 The Moment/Sunset   자수, 월넛, 백동, 정은, 스프레이 페인트 embroidery, walnut wood, nickel silver, sterling silver, spray paint
4.6×8.4×2.8cm   2024

유아미 Ahmi Yu

고요한 얼굴 Silk feels 유리비즈, 비단, 적동, 주석 glass beads, silk, copper, tin 13×13×2.5cm 2024

유아미 Ahmi Yu

바삭바삭한 하양 The blue object 청금석, 비단, 적동, 채색 lapis lazuli, silk, copper, paint 8.3×8×2cm 2024

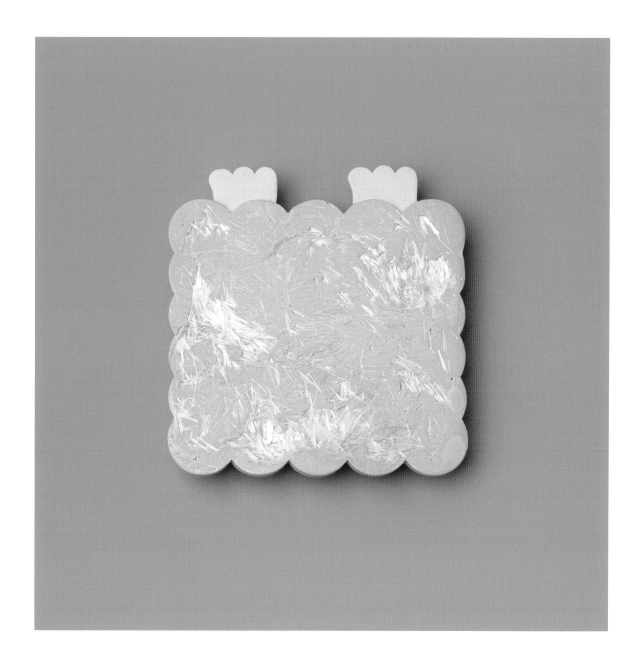

엄세희 Sehee Um

이불이 훔쳐간 것들 Things My Blanket Stole   제스모나이트, 유리섬유 jesmonite, fiber glass   10.5×11.2×3cm   2024

엄세희 Sehee Um

잠요정의 이불 Sandman's Covers
제스모나이트, 알루미나 jesmonite,
alumina 11.5×11×3cm 2024

김유정 Yoojung Kim

닭장 Hen House   호박, 레진, 퍼티, 정은 amber, resin, putty, sterling silver   7.3×8.8×0.8cm   2024

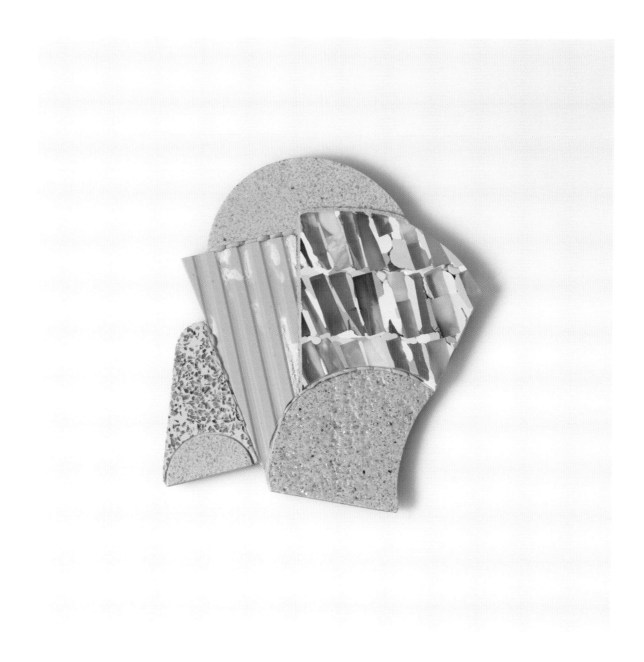

인공 폭포 Artificial Waterfall   호박, 레진, 퍼티, 정은 amber, resin, putty, sterling silver   8.4×9.3×0.8cm   2024

김지민 Jimin Kim

얇은분홍과 포도 palepinkgrape 한지, 나무, 정은 korean paper, wood, sterling silver 13×11×4.5cm 2024

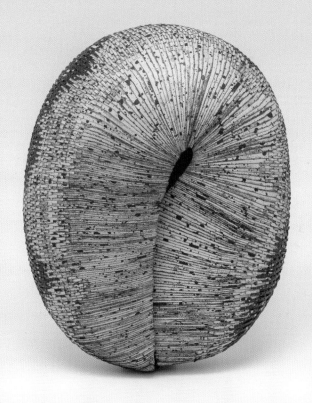

회녹 graypine   한지, 나무, 정은 korean paper, wood, sterling silver   9.5×12×4cm   2024

이승열 Sungyeoul Lee

겹쳐진 상 6 Overlapped form 6   정은, 스테인리스 스틸 sterling silver, stainless steel   10×10×3.5cm   2024

겹쳐진 상 7 Overlapped form 7   정은, 스테인리스 스틸 sterling silver, stainless steel   9.5×11×3.5cm   2024

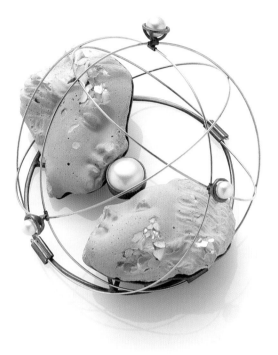

김아랑 Arang Kim

브로카와 베르니케 Broca and Wernicke 칼라시멘트, 정은, 자개, 진주, 스테인리스 스틸 선 color cement, sterling silver, mother of pearl, pearl, stainless steel wire 9×7×6cm 2024

기도 Pray   칼라시멘트, 정은, 진주 color cement, sterling silver, pearl   6×20×3cm   2024

김혜원 Hyewon Kim

심연 I Abyss I 레진, 스펀지 resin, sponge 7×11×5cm 2024

심연 II Abyss II   레진, 나무뿌리 resin, wood   10×15×5cm   2024

백시내 Sinae Baik

조용한 하루 Rest day   순은, 유리, 칠보 fine silver, glass, enamel   10.5×13×8cm   2024

조용한 하루 Rest day   순은, 유리, 칠보 fine silver, glass, enamel   11×13×8cm   2024

김민정 Minjeong Kim

1986 알루미늄, 금, 정은 aluminium, gold, sterling silver   7.5×8×1cm   2024

1986 알루미늄, 금, 정은 aluminium, gold, sterling silver   7.5×5×1cm   2024

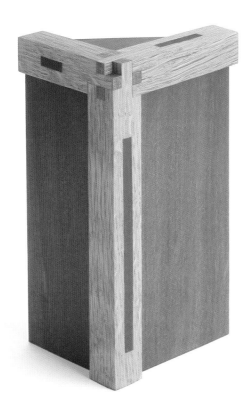

임제운 Jewoon Lim

맞추다 Pieces are joined 유창목, 백참나무, 정은 lignum vitae, white oak, sterling silver 7.5×11×4cm 2024

끼우다 Fitted into the piece 유창목, 백참나무, 정은 lignum vitae, white oak, sterling silver 6×10×4.5cm 2024

심진아 Jina Sim

제어 Control 스테인리스 스틸, 정은, 에나멜 와이어, 실 stainless steel, sterling silver, enamel wire, thread 13×32×10cm 2024

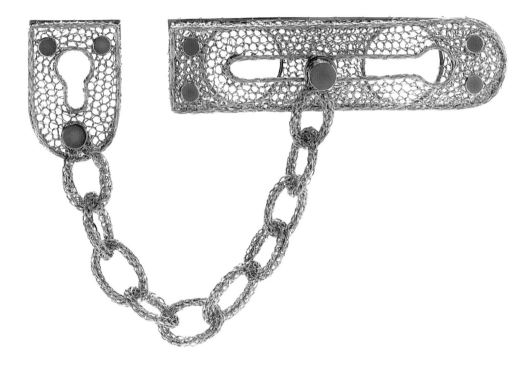

심진아 Jina Sim

장치 Device　스테인리스 스틸, 정은 stainless steel, sterling silver　16×11×2.5cm　2024

한은석 Eunseok Han

생성 I Becoming I 알루미늄 캔, PLA, HMA, 정은, 적동 aluminium can, PLA, HMA, sterling silver, copper 12×16×4cm 2024

한은석 Eunseok Han

생성 II Becoming II 알루미늄 캔, PLA, HMA, 정은, 적동 aluminium can, PLA, HMA, sterling silver, copper 10×18×4cm 2024

송유경 Yookyung Song

물결 속의 조각들 Fragments in Water
아크릴, 갈륨, 레진, 정은, 스테인리스 스틸
acrylic, gallium, resin, sterling silver,
stainless steel 9.5×8.5×1cm 2024

물결 속의 조각들 Fragments in Water   아크릴, 갈륨, 레진, 정은, 스테인리스 스틸 acrylic, gallium, resin, sterling silver, stainless steel
9×13×3cm   2024

이주현 Joohyun Lee

나무가 있는 모퉁이 Corner with tree 정은, 파덕나무 sterling silver, red wood 11.3×9.5×2cm 2024

나무와 모퉁이 Trees and corner   정은, 파덕나무 sterling silver, red wood   11.5×9.8×1cm   2024

윤지예 Jiye Yun
조각의 조각의 조각 I Parts of parts of parts I 레진, 퍼티, 스테인리스 스틸 photopolymer resin, putty, stainless steel 6×5.5×2.7cm 2024

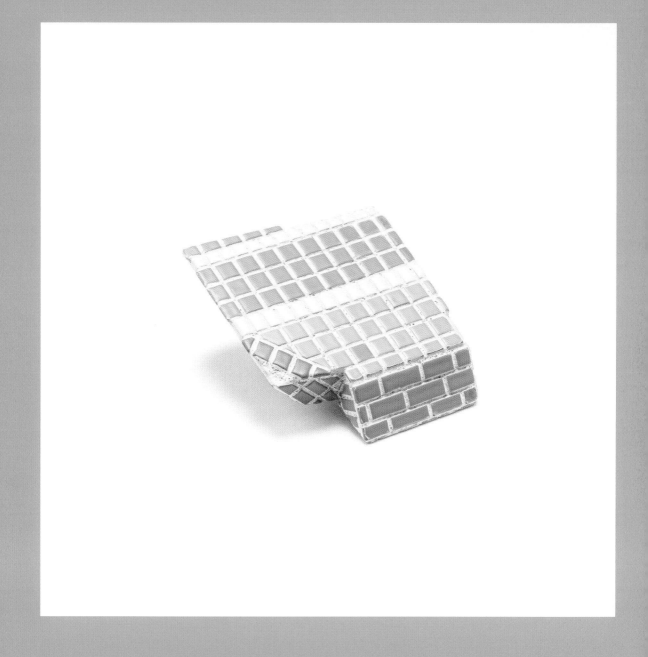

조각의 조각의 조각 II Parts of parts of parts II   레진, 퍼티, 스테인리스 스틸 photopolymer resin, putty, stainless steel   5.6×6.5×1.5cm   2024

서예슬 Yeseul Seo

자연의 초상_늑대 Portrait of nature_wolf 양모, 은행나무, 레진, 황동, 왁스 wool felt, ginkgo wood, resin, brass, wax 10×12×6cm 2024

자연의 초상_산양 Portrait of nature_mountain goat   양모, 호두나무, 레진, 황동, 왁스 wool felt, walnut wood, resin, brass, wax
9×11.5×7cm   2024

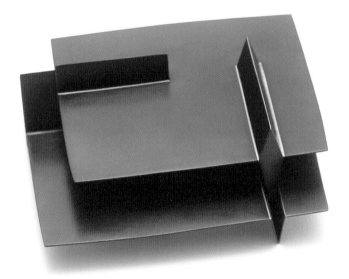

노은주 Eunjoo Noh

두 개의 브로치 Two Ornaments for Brooch   적동, 블랙C 착색 copper, black C   9.5×8.5×3.7cm   2024

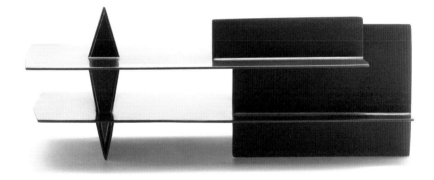

두 개의 브로치 Two Ornaments for Brooch   적동, 블랙C 착색 copper, black C   9.5×8.5×3.7cm   2024

김희앙 Hee-ang Kim

안과 밖 8 Inside out 8 폴리머클레이, 석분점토, 정은, 아크릴 페인트, 레진 polymer clay, stone clay, sterling silver, acrylic paint, resin
9.5×10×4.3cm   2024

피어나는 시간 3 Time to bloom 3   폴리머클레이, 석분점토, 정은, 아크릴 페인트 polymer clay, stone clay, sterling silver, acrylic paint
9×9.3×7.1cm   2024

한은지 Eunji Han

여름초록 Summer green 한지, 면사, 바다자개, 채색 korean paper, cotton yarn, mother of pearl, paint 7.5×19×5cm 2024

여름초록 Summer green   한지, 면사 korean paper, cotton yarn   8.5×10×4cm   2024

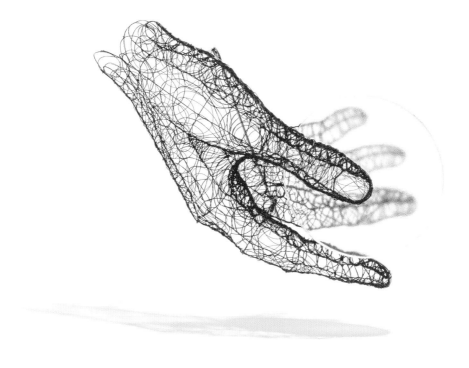

최혜영 Hyeyoung Choi

가벼운 Light 머리카락, 황동, 아크릴 human hair, brass, acrylic 8.8×6.5×2cm 2023

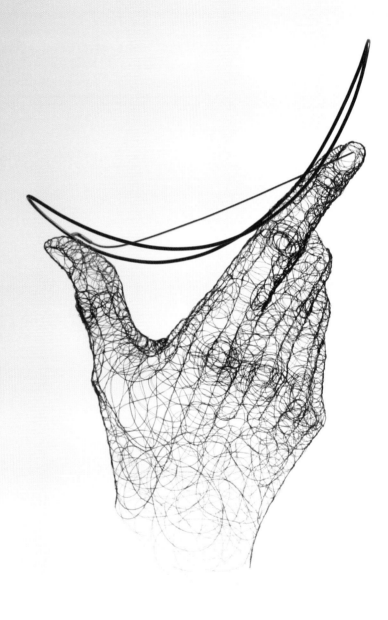

손길 Touch   머리카락, 황동 human hair, brass   10.5×17×2.5cm   2021

복합적 형식

브루스 멧칼프

시러큐스Syracus 대학교에서 금속을 전공하던 나는 1971년 2학기 때 처음으로
브로치를 만들었다. 그리 잘 만든 것은 아니었다. 그것은 하나의 작은 유리
방울이, 몇 개의 돌돌 말린 은으로 둘러싸여 있는 브로치였다. 나는 아르누보
양식을 염두하고 만들었지만 크게 실패하였다. 순조로운 시작은 아니었다.
내 기억이 맞는다면 그것을 여자 친구의 어머니에게 선물한 것 같다.

그 후 15년 동안 나는 조각 작업에 집중하였다. 아주 작은 조각 작업을 한다는
것이 좋지 않은 생각이었다는 것을 깨닫는 데 그만큼이나 오랜 시간이 걸렸다.
나는 가끔씩 장신구를 만들곤 했는데, 거의 브로치였다. 90년대 중반에 나는
조각 작업을 포기하고, 장신구 작업에 전념하기 시작하였다. 그 이후로 내가 만든
장신구는 대부분 브로치이다.

내 논리는 간단하다. 모든 유형의 장신구 중에서 브로치가 몸에 착용하기 위한
구조적 장치의 영향을 가장 적게 받는다. 브로치는 반지나 팔찌와 달리 고리나
그와 같은 형태가 따로 필요하지 않다. 또한 펜던트와 달리 체인이나 줄도
필요하지 않다. 그리고 목걸이와 달리 반복되는 유닛도 없다. 모든 구조적 장치는
보이지 않는 뒤쪽에 있다. 앞면에 내가 원하는 모든 것을 할 수 있다. 완벽하다.
모든 종류의 장신구 중에서, 형태와 이미지를 몸에 부착하기 위한 구조적
장치로부터 완전히 독립된 특성은 브로치에서만 볼 수 있다. 그래서 형태와
이미지를 제약 없이 자유롭게 표현할 수 있다. 나의 한 친구는 브로치를 휴대용
광고판이라고 불렀는데, 이는 사실과 크게 다르지 않다. 광고판에는 당신이 원하는
어떤 장면이든 만들 수가 있다.

하지만 브로치는 착용성으로 인한 현실적인 제약을 가지고 있다. 누군가는 순수 예술로 보여주기 위해 집채만 한 크기의 브로치를 만들 수도 있다. 하지만 그것을 착용하기 위해서는 너무 커도 안 되고, 너무 두꺼워도 안 되며, 너무 무거워도 안 된다. 브로치는 두께 10 밀리미터 범위를 유지해야 한다. 그렇지 않으면 자유로운 움직임에 방해가 될 수 있으며, 대부분의 사람들이 생각하는 상식의 범위에서 벗어날 수 있다. 이러한 이유에서 브로치의 두께는 꽤 얇아야 한다. 그리고 브로치를 단 옷감이 처지거나 늘어나지 않을 정도로 가벼워야 한다. 이처럼 브로치는 항상 크기에 제약을 받는다. 브로치는 손으로 쥘 수 있는 미니어처의 영역에 속한다.

많은 현대 예술가들은 미니어처에 대한 큰 거부감을 가지고 있다. 그들은 마치 모든 작은 사물들을 장난감 정도로 여기듯이, 작은 작업을 하는 것은 예술가로서 큰 포부가 없는 것이라고 치부한다. 하지만 그것은 사실이 아니다.

작은 것이야 말로 우리를 크게 만든다. 우리는 그 미니어처보다 훨씬 더 크지만 그것은 우리를 더 가까이 끌어당긴다. 그리고 가까이 다가갈수록 꿈을 꾸는 것과 같은 상태로 존재하는 작은 세계, 또 다른 우주로 우리를 유혹한다. 그 우주로 들어가려면 상상력을 발휘해야 한다. 그리고 그곳에는 크기에 대한 제약이 없다. 당신의 상상대로 만들어낸 세계로 들어가면, 크기는 더 이상 중요하지 않다. 인형의 집이나 기차 모형에 매료된 적이 있는 사람은 누구나 이러한 현상에 익숙할 것이다. 브로치를 들어 살펴보기 시작하면, 당신은 이러한 다른 세상으로 빠져들게 된다.

많은 사람들이 브로치를 작은 조각품이라고 말한다. 하지만 이는 잘못된 생각이다. 예술에서 브로치와 유사한 유형이 있다면 그것은 부조일 것이다. 브로치는 부조처럼 비교적 평평하지만 결코 간과되어서는 안될 뒷면이 존재한다. 여러 예술의 유형 중에서 브로치를 아주 특별하게 만드는 점이 바로 뒷면이 있다는 것이다.

부조, 그림, 소묘 또는 설치 작품의 뒷면을 보는 사람은 아무도 없지만, 브로치는 쉽게 뒤집어서 살펴볼 수 있다. 아마도 내가 아는 모든 장신구 작가들은 브로치를 집어 들면 앞면을 흘끗 본 다음, 바로 뒤집어서 뒷면을 볼 것이다. 여기다. 바로 여기서 흥미로운 점들이 드러난다.

모든 브로치는 앞면의 심미성과 뒷면의 구조적 장치를 어떻게 풀어나갈 지에 대한 난제를 해결해야 한다. 모든 브로치에는 핀과 핀 걸이 그리고 잠금 장치가 있다.

이 뒷면의 구조적 장치가 심미성이 중요한 앞면과 어떻게 어울릴 수 있을까?

앞면의 디자인 요소가 핀과 핀 걸이 그리고 잠금 장치와 유사한 경우는 드물다.
전면의 모습은 다른 언어로 표현된다. 따라서 개념이나 표현에 따른 구성과 평범하게
기능에 충실한 구성, 이 두 가지의 언어가 있다. 기본적으로 장신구 작가에게는
이 두 언어를 가능한 동일하게 만들거나, 이 둘은 근본적으로 분리되어 있음을
받아들이는 두 개의 선택지가 있다.

나는 작업에 있어서 후자를 따른다. 사실 나는 대부분 예술적인 것과는 거리가 먼
기성 제품인 핀 걸이와 잠금 장치를 사용한다. 순수한 기능만을 가진 것. 하지만
예술에 있어서 기능을 수행하는 장치에 대한 익숙한 비유가 있다. 기술적 장치를
드러내는 것은 예술 작품 뒤에 숨어있는 전략을 드러낸다는 것이다. 프로젝터와 다른
장비가 여러 전선들과 함께 끝없이 설치된 모습에서 이러한 사고를 엿볼 수 있는데,
이는 기기의 작동방식을 직설적으로 보여준다. 나는 이런 직설적인 방식을 좋아한다.

모든 브로치는 심미성과 기능적 장치 사이의 충돌을 수반한다. 브로치는 필연적으로
양면성을 가진다. 사실, 그 대비는 꽤 흥미로울 수 있다. 그것이 바로 브로치의
특징이다. 장신구 작가는 기능을 수행하는 장치가 브로치를 압도하지 않으면서도
역할을 잘 해내는 균형 잡힌 작업을 한다. 그렇지 않으면 매우 조화롭지 않게 보일 수
있다. 작가는 반드시 자신만의 취향과 독창성을 발휘해야 한다.

이러한 브로치는 또 다른 관점에서 설명할 수 있다. 브로치는 착용 시 다른 종류의
장신구와 달리 피부에 직접 닿지 않는다. 반지, 팔찌, 목걸이는 일반적으로 부분이나
전체가 피부에 닿아 촉감을 통해 그 존재를 느낄 수 있다. 하지만 브로치는 옷감에
달려 있어, 즉각적이고 감각적인 접촉은 불가능하다. 브로치는 신체와 직접적으로
연결되지 않는다. 그들은 서로 떨어져 있다.

많은 형태의 유용한 공예품은 우리 몸에 자연스레 닿고, 또 우리는 그것들을 만진다.
도자기 그릇, 가구, 의류, 도구, 그리고 대부분의 장신구는 모두 사용자와 직접적으로
접촉한다. 그 결과 대부분의 순수 예술이 줄 수 없는 다양하고 즐거운 경험을
선사한다. 박물관에 있는 그림, 소묘, 판화, 그리고 조각품은 어떨까?
그 곁에는 모두 "만지지 마세요."라는 안내문이 붙어 있고, 이것은 예술품의
상업적인 역할을 의미한다. 너무 가까이 다가가면 경보가 울린다. 여기서 소위

브루스 멧칼프 Bruce Metcalf　장신구의 알레고리 #51 Allegories of Jewelry #51　브로치 앞면／뒷면　front／back side of brooch
단풍나무 조각, 채색 carved and painted maple　8.7×6.8cm　2023

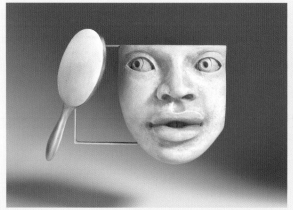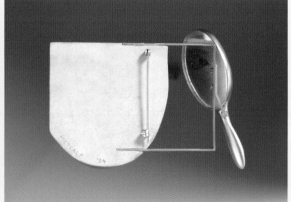

브루스 멧칼프 Bruce Metcalf　장신구의 알레고리 #63 Allegories of Jewelry #63　브로치 앞면／뒷면　front／back side of brooch
단풍나무 조각, 채색, 정은, 거울 아크릴 carved and painted maple, sterling silver, mirror plexiglass　5.4×8.2cm　2024

말하는 **미적 경험**은 볼 수 있는 것, 그리고 때로는 들을 수 있는 것에만 국한되어 있다. 대부분의 경우 직접적인 신체적 경험과 관련된 모든 것은 제한된다.

그래서 예술품은 멀리 떨어져 닿을 수 없는 곳인 전용 전시대 위에 있다. 이것이 작품과의 교감을 저하시키는 꽤 안타까운 경험이 될 것이라고 상상하기는 어렵지 않다. 우리가 삶에서 가장 즐기는 것의 대부분은 전신과 관련이 있다. 음악을 듣기만 하는 것이 아니라 춤을 추는 것, 문자로 읽기만 하는 것이 아니라 의식을 행하는 것, 보기만 하는 것뿐만 아니라 만져보는 것까지. "보기만 하고 만지지 마시오."라는 원칙은 꽤 지겨울 수 있다.

브로치를 달면 몸에 직접 닿지 않는다고 해도, 우리는 그것을 착용하고 뺄 때에 여전히 만져볼 수 있다. 브로치를 착용할 때마다 그것을 들어 무게와 질감을 느껴보고, 견고함을 판단한 다음, 핀 장식을 옷감에 끼우고 잠금 장치를 닫는다. 이 과정은 즐거울 수도 있고 답답할 수도 있지만, 손과 사물 사이를 밀접하게 해주는 촉각이 강하게 작용한다.

브로치를 만지고, 옷에 다는 과정은 몸을 다시 한번 감각적으로 경험하게 한다. 이 경험은 단순히 보는 것보다 더 복합적이고 다채롭다. 이곳에, 우리를 육체적 세계로 회귀시켜주는 예술 형식이 있다. 한 번에 며칠씩 컴퓨터 앞에 앉아 있는 사람이라면 누구나, 신체적 경험을 다시 한다는 것의 가치를 알 수 있을 것이다. 나는 손에 쥐어 보지 않은 브로치는 실제로 완성되지 않은 것이라 생각한다. 브로치를 만지며 다루어 보는 경험은, 그것을 착용했을 때 느끼는 거리감을 상쇄시킨다.

브로치에 대한 촉각적 경험은 그것의 시각적 성향을 보완해준다. 우리는 그림을 감상할 때처럼 브로치를 온전한 시각적 독립체로 즐기게 되고, 그것을 하나의 사고가 실현된 개념으로 여기게 된다. 게다가 브로치를 손에 쥐는 경험은 이 모든 과정을 더욱 풍요롭게 한다. 우리는 그것에 대해 생각할 수 있을 뿐만 아니라, 느낄 수 있게 된다.

브로치나 다른 장신구를 손으로 다루어 보는 경험은 그것이 만들어지는 과정을 재현하는 것이다. 브로치를 3D 프린터로 만들지 않은 이상, 작가는 몇 시간, 며칠, 심지어 몇 주 동안 손으로 붙잡고 있었을 것이다. 실질적일 뿐만 아니라

은유적으로도 작가의 지문은 브로치 곳곳에 남아 있다. 브로치는 두 손으로부터
시작된다. 그 구석구석에 작가의 손길이 닿아, 노동과 보살핌의 대상이 된다.
그리고 착용자는 브로치를 만질 때마다 제작자의 손길을 재현하며 지난 제작
과정을 되풀이한다.

모든 장신구와 마찬가지로 브로치도 몸에 착용한 후에는 두 가지의 방향을 가지게
된다. 브로치의 한 면은 착용한 것을 보는 모든 사람을 향해 바깥쪽을 향하고, 다른
한 면은 착용자를 향해 안쪽을 향한다.

장신구를 착용하는 것은 매우 사회적인 행동이다. 우리는 진실 혹은 허구일 수 있는
자신에 대한 이야기를 전달하기 위해 장신구를 착용한다. 그렇다, 장신구는 거짓말을
할 수 있다! 사람들은 그 이야기를 인지한 다음, 보이는 것을 바탕으로 스스로 판단을
내린다. 장신구는 기호학적 관점에서 기호이면서 의미일 수 있지만, 그보다 더
복잡할 수도 있다.

예를 들어, 장신구는 공통점과 차이점에 대한 메시지를 각각 전달할 수 있으며,
때로는 두 가지를 동시에 전달할 수도 있다. 구부정한 자세로 면도날을 장신구로
하고 다니는 원조 영국 펑크족을 생각해 보자. 그들에게 면도날은 정통 영국
중산층의 미덕에 대한 거부를 의미했지만, 또 다른 펑크족에게는 같은 가치를
공유하는 집단의 일원임을 의미했다. 이렇게 장신구는 어딘가 소속되어 있음과
그렇지 않음을 동시에 전달할 수 있다. 나는 이곳에 속해 있지만 저곳에 속해 있지
않다는 두 사실을 장신구를 통해 공개적으로 알릴 수 있는 것이다.

또한 장신구는 분명히 지위, 부, 권력, 영성, 마력 등을 포함해 그 이상에 대한
정보를 전달한다. 이 모든 것은 장신구가 관중을 마주하고 소통한다는 것을
의미한다.

하지만 이는 이야기의 절반에 불과하다. 장신구는 착용자 역시 그 정보로부터
영향을 받게 한다.

장신구 작가인 로버트 리 모리스Robert Lee Morris와 고인이 된 샤론 처치 Sharon
Church는 장신구가 어떻게 자아를 변화시킬 수 있는지에 대해 이야기했다. 처치는
사회생활에서 겪는 시련을 막아주는 정신적 방어막으로의 장신구를 말했다.

모리스도 이와 같은 맥락에서 장신구로 자기를 관리하고 치장하는 데서 얻는 치유력에 대해 이야기했다. 우리는 어떤 장신구를 착용하는 지에 따라, 스스로에 대한 생각을 바꾸어 더 자신감 있고, 더 아름답고, 더 갖추어진 느낌을 가질 수 있다.

브로치는 기능적으로 고려해야할 사항에 얽매이지 않고, 폭넓은 이미지를 담을 수 있기 때문에 이러한 역할을 하기에 특히나 적절하다. 브로치가 가진 더 많은 자유를 통해 자기 관리와 정신적인 방어막 등을 포함한 폭넓은 역할을 잘 수행할 수 있다.

전직 장신구 작가였던 한 친구는 "장신구는 작은 전달 수단이다."라고 말한 적이 있다. 그녀는 장신구 작업을 하기에는 자신의 야망이 너무 커서 회화와 조각으로 전향해야 한다는 뜻이었다. 그녀의 말이 맞을까? 글쎄. 나는 거의 지난 50년 동안 꾸준히 브로치를 만들어 왔고, 브로치가 나의 야망을 담기에 꼭 알맞다고 자신 있게 말할 수 있다. 나는 작은 것들로 이루어진 세계를 좋아한다. 나는 앞과 뒤의 이분법을 좋아한다. 나는 착용하기 전 브로치를 손에 쥐어야 하는 것을 좋아한다. 나는 브로치를 옷의 어디에, 어떻게 고정시킬 지를 생각하게 만드는 과정을 좋아한다. 나는 브로치가 사회 속에서 자신을 드러내는 방식과 우리가 자신에 대해 말하는 데 그것을 사용하는 방식을 좋아한다.

브로치는 복잡한 예술 양식이다. 브로치는 여러 면에서 모순적인 속성을 가지고 있다. 앞/뒷면. 접촉/접촉하지 않음. 진실/거짓. 바깥쪽/안쪽. 브로치는 **둘 중 하나/ 또는**이 아닌 **둘 다/그리고**라는 의미에서 모순들을 포용한다. 이것이 만약 브로치의 한계라면, 나는 그 한계와 더불어 아주 행복하게 살 수 있다.

브루스 멧칼프는 1972년 시라큐스 대학교에서 학사 학위를, 1977년 필라델피아 타일러 미술대학에서 석사 학위를 받았다. 두 번의 NEA 시각예술 펠로우십, 세 번의 오하이오 미술협회 펠로우십, 한국 문화연구를 위한 풀브라이트 펠로우십, Pew 미술분야 펠로우십을 받았다. 그의 장신구는 전 세계 400개 이상의 전시회에 출품되었으며, 메트로폴리탄 미술관, 필라델피아 미술관, 런던의 빅토리아 앤 앨버트 박물관, 워싱턴 DC의 렌윅 갤러리 등 수많은 공공 컬렉션에 소장되어 있다. 멧칼프는 자넷 코플로스와 「제작자: 미국 스튜디오 공예의 역사」의 공동 저자이다. 그는 미국 필라델피아 근처에 거주하고 있다.

A Complex Form

Bruce Metcalf

I made my first brooch in 1971, during my second semester as a metals student at Syracuse University. It was not very good. It consisted of a blob of glass among a few curls of silver. I was probably thinking about Art Nouveau, but I missed the mark by a wide margin. Not an auspicious beginning. If memory serves me right, I gave it to my girlfriend's mother.

For the next fifteen years, I concentrated on making sculptures. It took me that long to figure out that teeny sculptures are a bad idea. I would make jewelry once in a while, and when I did, it was almost always a brooch. By the mid 90s, I gave up on the sculpture project, and turned to jewelry full-time. Ever since, most of jewelry I make are brooches.

My logic is simple: of all the forms of jewelry, the brooch is least controlled by the mechanics of getting the thing on the body. No loops, unlike rings and bracelets. No chains or strings, unlike pendants. No repeated elements, unlike necklaces. All the mechanics are out of sight, exiled to the back. On the front, I can do whatever I wanted. Perfect.

Among all types of jewelry, the property of form and image being utterly independent of the mechanics of attaching the object to the body is found only in brooches. Form and image can run riot, uncompromised. A friend of mine once called brooches **portable billboards**, and that's not far from the truth. The billboard can look like anything you want.

However, practical limits are imposed by wearability. I suppose one could, in the service of high art, make a brooch the size of a house. But if the brooch is to be worn, then it can't be too big, it can't be too thick, and it can't be too heavy. Brooches must remain small, in the range of 10 millimeter of so. Otherwise they interfere with free movement, and would probably offend most people's sense of propriety. They have to be fairly shallow, for the same reasons. And they have to be light enough not to sag or stretch the fabric upon which they are suspended. Thus, brooches are always constrained by scale. Brooches live in the realm of the miniature, something that can be held in the hand.

Many contemporary artists have a great revulsion for the miniature. They find the very small to be a sign of low ambition, as if all small things were playthings. That is not true.

Small things make us large. We tower over the miniature but are drawn closer. And the closer we get, the more we are seduced into a world in small, a parallel universe that exists in a dreamlike state. To enter that universe, you must use your imagination. And in the, there is no scale. You enter a world created by your own mind, and size no longer matters. Anyone who has been enchanted by a dollhouse or a model train layout knows how this phenomenon works. When you pick up a brooch and begin to investigate, you are drawn into that other realm.

A lot of people say brooches are small sculptures. They are wrong. If there is a resemblance to an art form, it is to reliefs. Brooches are relatively flat, just like reliefs, and but brooches also have a back, which cannot be ignored. It is this business of always having a back that make brooches unique among art forms.

While nobody ever looks at the back of a relief. Or a painting. Or a drawing. Or an installation. But it's a simple matter to turn a brooch over and take a look. Every jeweler I know will do this: they'll pick a brooch up, glance at the front, and immediately flip it over to look at the back. There it is. What you see is quite revealing.

All brooches face a conundrum: how do the mechanics relate to the aesthetics of the front? Every brooch has a joint, a pin stem, and a catch. How do these tiny mechanisms compare to the front, where the aesthetics live?

It's rare for the design elements of the front to resemble the joint, stem, or catch. The visuals on the front are a different language. Thus you have a composition that is speaking in two tongues, one driven by concept or expression, and the other by prosaic function. Basically, the jeweler has two choices: make the two languages as much the same as possible, or just accept a fundamental discontinuity.

In my practice, I accept the discontinuity. In fact, I generally use commercial joints and catches, which aren't even remotely arty. Pure function. However, there is a familiar trope in art about mechanics: revealing the technology is a reminder of the artifice behind the work of art. You can see that mentality in endless installations where projectors and other equipment sit in the midst of coils of wires: a blunt reminder how the thing works. I'm all for the blunt reminder.

Every brooch must encompass the conflict between aesthetics and mechanisms. There's an inevitable two-sidedness that comes with the form. In fact, the contrast can be pretty interesting. It's part of being a brooch. The jeweler performs a balancing act: accommodating mechanisms without allowing them to overpower. Or for that matter, to look too weird. One must exercise taste and ingenuity.

That sense of the brooch being bifurcated continues into other areas. When worn, a brooch never touches the skin, unlike most other forms of jewelry. Rings, bracelets, necklaces: generally, they lie wholly or partly on the skin, heightening their presence through touch. But brooches hang on fabric, insulated from immediate sensual contact. Brooches lack that unmediated connection to the body. They sit apart.

Many forms of useful craft get to touch us, and we get to touch them. Pots, furniture, garments, tools, and most forms of jewelry all come into direct contact with their users. The result is a complex and pleasurable experience that most fine art cannot provide. All those paintings, drawings, prints and sculptures in museums? They are accompanied by "Do not touch" signs, and those guys mean business. Get too close and an alarm goes off. The so-called **aesthetic experience** is limited to what you can see, and sometimes to what you can hear. Most of the time, anything pertaining to direct bodily experience is off limits.

So art sits on its pedestal, deracinated and remote. It doesn't take too much imagination to think that this experience is impoverished and rather sad. So much of what we most enjoy about living involves the whole body. Not just the music but the dancing, not just the text but the ritual, not just the seeing but the touching. The doctrine of "look-but-do-not-touch" can get pretty tiresome.

If the brooch does not touch the body when worn, we still get to handle it when we put it on and take it off. Any time you wear a brooch, you pick it up, feel its weight and texture, judge its firmness, and then insert the pin stem into fabric and close the catch. This process may be pleasurable or it may be frustrating, but it is intensely haptic, a close relation between hand and object.

Handling the brooch, putting the brooch on clothing: both offer a sensuous experience that brings the body back into the equation. The experience is more complex and richer than mere seeing. Here, you have an artform that returns us to the physical world. And anybody who has sat at a computer for days at a time might see the virtue of a return to the physical.

A brooch that is never held in the hand is, in my estimation, unfulfilled. The experience of handling a brooch balances out its remoteness when worn.

The haptic experience of a brooch also compliments its visual nature. We get to see the brooch, enjoy it strictly as a visual entity, exactly as we might enjoy a painting. We get to consider it as a concept, as an exercise in thought. But we also experience the brooch in the hand, which enriches the entire process. We can think about it, but we get to feel it too.

The experience of handling a brooch – or any piece of jewelry, for that matter – replays the process of its making. As long as the brooch is not a 3-D print, the jeweler spent hours, days, or even weeks, holding the thing in their hands. The jeweler's fingerprints are all over the thing, in actuality and in metaphor. The brooch began its life in a pair of hands: every square millimeter has been touched. It becomes a receptacle of labor and care. And whenever a brooch is touched, the wearer re-enacts the touch of the maker, replicating the process of making.

Like all jewelry, a brooch also has a bifurcated nature after it is placed on the body. The brooch faces outward, towards all who see it worn, as well as inward, towards its wearer.

Wearing jewelry is deeply social. We wear jewelry to tell a story about ourselves, which can be truth or fiction. Yes, jewelry can lie! People perceive that story, and then make decisions for themselves based on what they see. Jewelry can be semiotic - sign and signified - but it can be more complicated than that.

For instance, jewelry can convey messages about sameness and difference, and sometimes both at the same time. Think about the original British punks, slouching about, wearing razor blades. The blade signified a rejection of proper British middle-class virtues, but to another punk, it signified a member of the tribe, one with shared values. Jewelry can simultaneously communicate both belonging and not-belonging. I belong here, but I don't belong there, and my jewelry is a public announcement of both.

Obviously, jewelry also conveys information about status, wealth, power, spirituality, magic, and much more. All this is jewelry facing outward to its audience, communicating meaning.

But that's only half the story. Jewelry reflects information back to its wearer. The jewelers Robert Lee Morris and the late Sharon Church both talked about how jewelry can alter one's sense of self. Church spoke of jewelry as psychic armor: a defense against the trials of social life. Morris talked about the healing power of self-care and adornment, which he saw as much the same thing. What we wear can alter what we think of ourselves, making us feel more confident, more beautiful, more prepared.

Brooches are particularly well-situated to do these jobs because they can accommodate such a wide range of imagery, untrammeled by functional considerations. With more freedom, brooches are better able to do the work of self-care, of psychic armoring, and much more.

An ex-jeweler friend of mine once said, "Jewelry is a small vehicle." What she meant is that she felt her ambitions were too big for jewelry, and she had to move up to painting and sculpture. Is she right? I don't know. I have been making brooches steadily for almost 50 years, and I can say with confidence that brooches suit my ambitions just fine. I like that world in small. I like that dichotomy of front and back. I like the way brooches sit in the hand. I like how a brooch invites you to fix it to your clothing. I like the way brooches get caught up in social life, and the way we use them to say things about ourselves.

The brooch is a complicated artform. They are bifurcated in many ways, encompassing contradictory properties. Front/back. Touch/not touch. Truth/lies. Outward/inward. The brooch embraces contradiction, in the spirit of **both/and** rather than **either/or**. If these are limitations, well, I can live with them quite happily.

Bruce Metcalf received a BFA from Syracuse University in 1972 and an MFA from Tyler School of Art in Philadelphia in 1977. He has been awarded two NEA Visual Artists Fellowships, three Ohio Arts Council Fellowships, a Fulbright Teaching and Research Fellowship for study in Korea, and a Pew Fellowship in the Arts. His jewelry has been shown in more than 400 exhibitions worldwide. It is held in numerous public collections, including the Metropolitan Museum of Art, the Philadelphia Museum of Art, the Victoria and Albert Museum in London and the Renwick Gallery in Washington, D.C. Metcalf is also co-author with Janet Koplos of 「Makers: A History of American Studio Craft」. He lives near Philadelphia, in the USA.

브로치

BROOCHES

이재현 Jaehyun Lee

안분지족(安分知足)_1 Happiness_1 정은, 백동, 종이점토, 한지, 차보라이트, 토파즈 큐빅 sterling silver, nickel silver, paper clay, korean paper, tsavorite, topaz cubic 10×15×4cm 2024

안분지족(安分知足)_2 Happiness_2   정은, 백동, 종이점토, 한지, 다이아몬드, 진주 sterling silver, nickel silver, paper clay, korean paper, diamond, pearl   10×12×5cm   2024

최예진 Ye-jin Choi
피어나다 1 Blossom 1   슈링클스, 파스텔, 정은 shrinkles, pastel, sterling silver   6.2×13×2.6cm   2024

피어나다 2 Blossom 2   슈링클스, 파스텔, 정은 shrinkles, pastel, sterling silver   8×13×2.3cm   2024

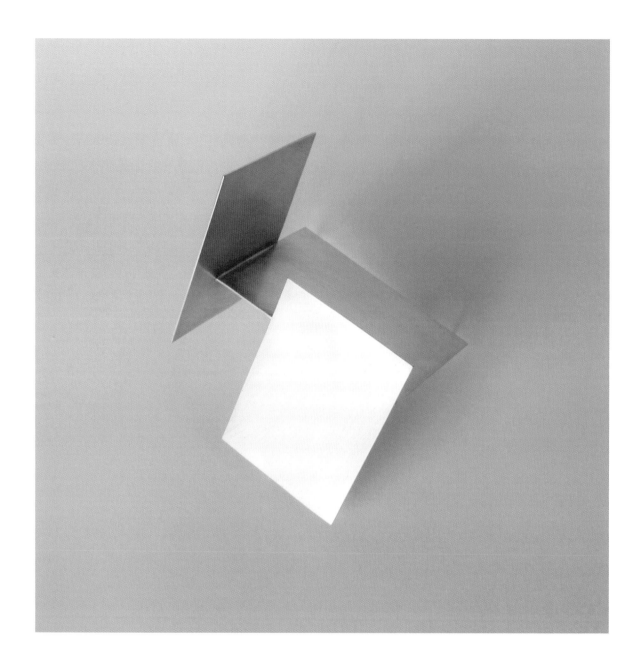

이소리 Sohri Yi

지어져가는 Being built 정은 sterling silver 7.5×9.8×8.6cm 2024

지어져가는 Being built 정은 sterling silver 7.3×8.5×6.5cm 2024

서은영　Eunyoung Seo

지나간 모든 시간, 다가 올 모든 시간 every moment that passed, every moment that will come　철, 정은, 백자 iron, sterling silver, ceramic
7.4×13.5×3.2cm　2024

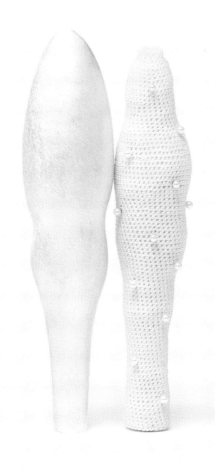

기억의 잎맥은 선명해진다 Leaf vein of memory, becomes clear   정은, 인노릴사, 진주 sterling silver, thread, pearl   5.8×13.5×3.1cm   2024

이남경 Namkyung Lee

순간들 Moments   정은, 사진, 아크릴 sterling silver, photograph, acrylic 8×11.2×4.5cm 2024

순간들 Moments   정은, 사진, 아크릴 sterling silver, photograph, acrylic   8.5×13.4×4.5cm   2024

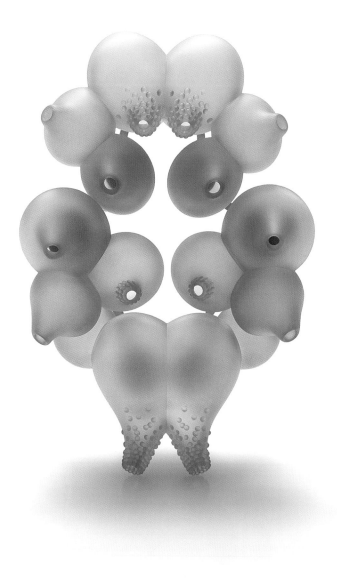

최윤정 Yoonjung Choi

숨시리즈_밸런스 #S015 Breath series_balanced #S015   특수 플라스틱, 정은, 3D 프린팅 special plastic, sterling silver, 3D printing
8×13×4.4cm   2024

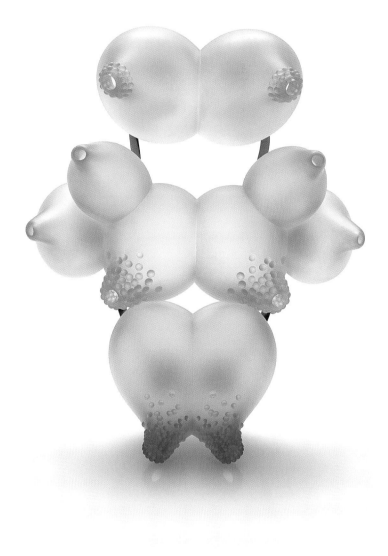

숨시리즈_밸런스 #S016 Breath series_balanced #S016　특수 플라스틱, 정은, 3D 프린팅 special plastic, sterling silver, 3D printing
9×11×4.4cm　2024

임종석 Jongseok Lim

계절은 지나가고 The seasons pass by   순은, 정은, 백동, 금박, 옻칠 fine silver, sterling silver, nickel silver, gold leaf, ottchil 12×13×3.5cm 2024

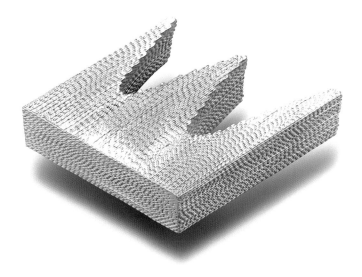

임종석 Jongseok Lim

형태는 남는다 Traces remain 순은, 정은 fine silver, sterling silver   10.5×7.5×1.5cm   2024

이진경 Jinkyung Lee

숨 **Breath**   실리콘, 실크, 실, 티타늄 silicon, silk, string, titanium   10×15×6cm   2024

이진경 Jinkyung Lee

흐름 Flow 실리콘, 실크, 실, 티타늄 silicon, silk, string, titanium 11×15×6cm 2024

민준석 Junsuk Min
롤링_브로치_2024 No.1 Rolling_Brooch_2024 No.1 정은, 합성루비, 황동 sterling silver, synthetic ruby, brass 6×6×1cm 2024

롤링_브로치_2024 No.2 Rolling_Brooch_2024 No.2   정은, 프린트 레진, 합성루비, 황동 sterling silver, printed resin, synthetic ruby, brass
6×6×1cm   2024

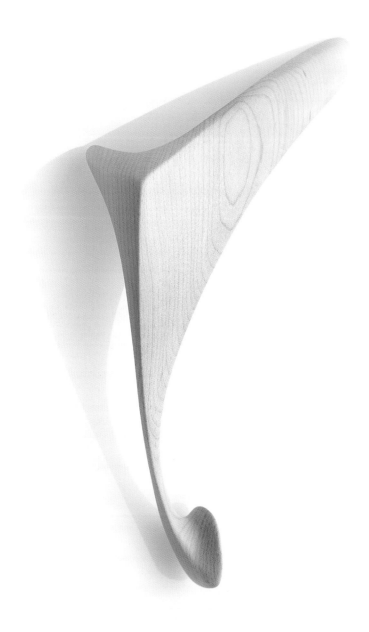

이형찬 Hyungchan Lee

No.8 하드메이플, 정은 hardmaple, sterling silver 12×14.5×4cm   2024

남겨둔 공간 A space set side 하드메이플, 정은 hardmaple, sterling silver 9.5×18×3cm 2024

진유리 Yuri Jin

2024년 6월의 브로치 1 RJ2406_1 면사, 솜, 황동 cotton yarn, cotton, brass 12×15.5×6cm 2024

2024년 6월의 브로치 2 RJ2406_2 면사, 황동 cotton yarn, brass 9×10.5×4cm 2024

김한나 Hanna Kim

기묘한 끌개 6 Strange Attractor 6   에폭시 레진, 정은 epoxy resin, sterling silver   10×13×4cm   2024

기묘한 끌개 7 Strange Attractor 7   에폭시 레진, 정은 epoxy resin, sterling silver   9×13×5cm   2024

원재선 Jaesun Won

축적된 시간 B20 Accumulated time B20 정은, 스테인리스 스틸, 실 sterling silver, stainless steel, thread 7.8×7.8×3.3cm 2024

축적된 시간 B19 Accumulated time B19   정은, 스테인리스 스틸, 실 sterling silver, stainless steel, thread   8.7×8.7×3.5cm   2024

박영빈 Youngbin Park

고살리 숲_1 Gosalli forest_1 정은, 사파이어, 다이아몬드 sterling silver, sapphire, diamond 4.5×6.5×1.5cm 2024

고살리 숲_2 Gosalli forest_2 정은, 금부, 사파이어, 다이아몬드 sterling silver, keum-boo, sapphire, diamond 3.5×8×1.5cm 2024

현성환 Seong-hwan Hyun

두 개의 달 **The two moons**   실, 황동, 금도금 thread, brass, gold plated   10×7.5×1.2cm   2024

현성환 Seong-hwan Hyun

파란 잎 Blue leaf 실, 정은 thread, sterling silver 9.5×7×2cm 2024

양지원 Jiwon Yang

비파리타 비라바드라아사나 Viparita Virabhadrasana   순은, 정은, 백동, 다이아몬드 fine silver, sterling silver, nickel silver, diamond
6.3×6.4×0.8cm   2024

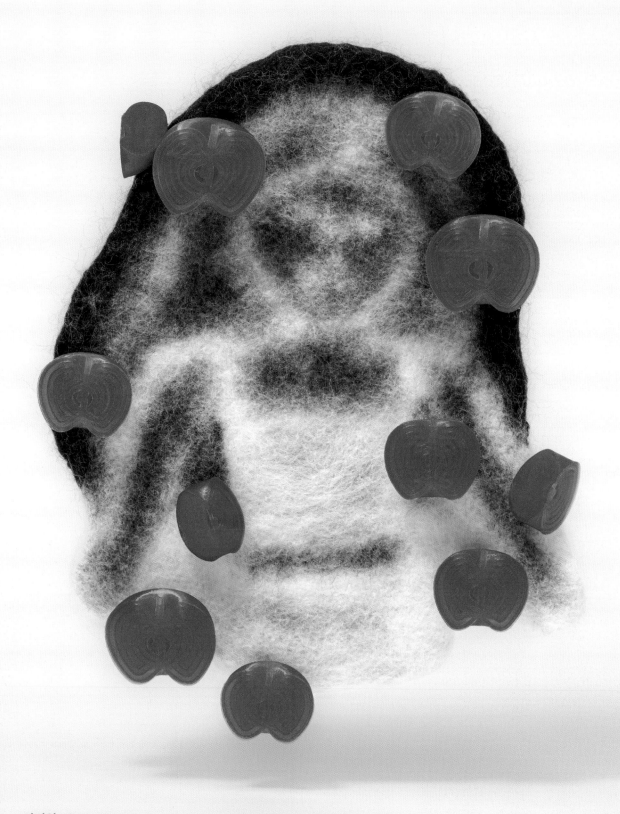

양지원 Jiwon Yang

사바아사나 Savasana 양모, 수지, 정은, 실 wool, PLA, sterling silver, thread 18×22×3cm 2024

홍예인 Yein Hong

난 괜찮아 I'm okay 황동, 금도금, 아크릴, 레진, 유성잉크 brass, gold plated, acrylic, resin, oil based ink 12×10×2cm 2024

띨래야 뗄 수 없는 사이 Can't be separated   황동, 금도금, 아크릴, 아세테이트판, 레진, 유성 잉크 brass, gold plated, acrylic, acetate sheet, resin, oil based ink   9×12×1cm   2024

이선용 Seonyong Lee

진화된 허물 Evolved cast skin   실리콘, 스테인리스 스틸 silicone, stainless steel   11×14×5.5cm   2024

진화된 허물 2 Evolved cast skin 2   실리콘, 스테인리스 스틸 silicone, stainless steel   10.5×11×5.5cm   2024

엄민재 Min-jae Eom

낙하점#1 Drop#1 순은, 정은 fine silver, sterling silver   7.5×7.5×1cm   2024

낙하점#2 Drop#2 순은, 정은 fine silver, sterling silver   7.5×7.5×1cm   2024

이나진 Najin Lee

크게 자라나는 마음 A growing heart 적동, 순은, 칠보, 라피스라줄리, 산호, 래브라도라이트, 금도금 copper, fine silver, enamel, lapis lazuli, coral, labradorite, gold plated 12.7×12.5×2cm 2024

가장 달콤한 말 A sweetest words   적동, 순은, 칠보, 자개, 진주, 금도금 copper, fine silver, enamel, mother of pearl, pearl, gold plated
10×11.5×2cm   2024

조완희 Wanhee Cho

환영의 투사 1 Projection of Illusion 1 레진, 정은 resin, sterling silver 12×10.5×7.5cm 2024

환영의 투사 2 Projection of Illusion 2   레진, 정은 resin, sterling silver   11×11×6cm   2024

엄유진 Youjin Um

회전목마 Merry Go Round   정은 sterling silver   11.5×5.2×2.4cm   2024

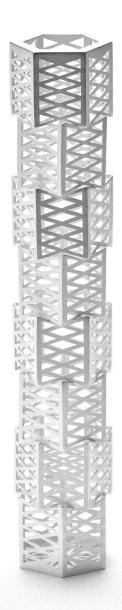

증식 Multiplication   정은 sterling silver   2.8×14.7×2.5cm   2024

장지영 Jiyoung Jang

눈 Bud   정은, 적동, 백자, 칠보 sterling silver, copper, porcelain, enamel   5×11×3cm   2024

식물 **Plant** 정은, 적동, 칠보 sterling silver, copper, enamel 7×12×2cm 2024

성코코 Coco Sung

나르시스트가 되지 않기 위한 노력 – 찰리 브라운 Trying not to be a narcissist – Charlie Brown   황동, 거울, 스왈로브스키 스톤, 비즈, 실, 점토, 채색
brass, mirror, swarovski stone, beads, thread, clay, paint   10.8×10.8×5.5cm   2024

나르시스트가 되지 않기위한 노력 – 틴틴 Trying not to be a narcissist – Tin Tin 백동, 황동, 거울, 스왈로브스키 스톤, 비즈, 실, 점토, 채색 nickel silver, brass, mirror, swarovski stone, beads, thread, clay, paint 11.8×11.8×6cm 2024

유다흰 Dahin Yoo

당신의 심장을 주세요 Give Me Your Heart 정은, 색박, 비즈, 크리스탈, PVC, 실 sterling sliver, colored silver leaf, beads, crystal, PVC, thread
7.5×10.5×3cm   2024

비상하는 꿈 Soaring Dream 정은, 색박, 비즈, TPU, 실 sterling silver, colored silver leaf, beads, TPU, thread 16×17.5×2.5cm 2024

덕후 The Koo 의 세계

현대예술장신구 컬렉터 성장기

구혜원

컬렉터collector란 특정 분야에 대한 열정과 흥미를 바탕으로 대상을 꾸준히
체계적으로 수집하고 관리하는 사람을 의미한다. 컬렉팅collecting은 단순히
소장하는 행위를 넘어 컬렉터의 취향과 안목, 가치관을 반영하여 하나의
컬렉션collection을 구축하는 일이다. 컬렉팅의 과정에서 즉흥적이고 감성적인
만족감을 얻는 것을 물론, 나아가 작업이나 작가에 대해 심도 있는 이해를 쌓는
것이 컬렉터의 핵심 역량이 된다.

컬렉팅이라는 행위를 통해 컬렉터와 작가는 소장자와 창작자라는 일차적 개념을
넘어서 유기적으로 긴밀하게 연결되는 공생의 관계를 형성한다. 가치 있는 예술
작품을 탄생시키는 데는 작가의 수준 높은 창작 활동이 중요하다. 컬렉터는
이 작품의 예술성을 인지하고, 평가하고, 구매함으로써 작품을 수집·보존하는
것은 물론, 작가가 계속해서 작품 활동을 하도록 발전의 원동력을 제공한다.
컬렉터의 행동은 예술가의 삶에 개입해 새로운 에너지를 불어 넣고, 예술가는
자신의 작업으로 컬렉터의 일상을 다시 변화시킨다. 이런 선순환적인 피드백을
통해 컬렉터와 작가는 서로 영향을 주며 성장하고, 동시대 문화의 흐름과 틀을
바꾸며 예술의 역사를 함께 만들어 나간다.

내가 컬렉터의 길로 들어선 것은 전적으로 초등학교 때부터의 친구인 김정후
작가의 공이다. 고등학교 때 느닷없이 미술을 전공하겠다고 깜짝 선언한 친구는
대학 졸업 후 유학길에 올랐다. 김정후 작가는 1989년 귀국하자마자 현대장신구
공모전에서 대상을 받았고, 나는 친구의 수상을 축하하고 작품을 관람하고자
워커힐미술관을 찾았다. 당시 현대예술장신구 분야엔 문외한이었던 내 눈에도

세상에 하나밖에 없는 개성 있고 독특한
장신구는 놀라웠고, 잠재되어 있던 예술적
호기심을 자극했다. 그 후 친구에게 나만을
위한 장신구를 주문하기에 이르렀다.
처음 주문할 때는 예술장신구 착용이
부담스러웠던 초보 컬렉터답게 가급적 작고,
튀지 않고, 단정한 수트에 어울리는 단순한
형태를 요구했던 것이 기억난다.

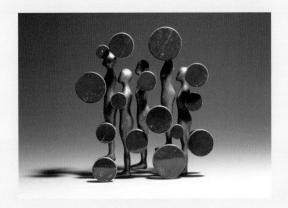

김정후 Junghoo Kim   물방울 15 The Waterdrops 15
브로치 brooch 정은, 라피스 라줄리 sterling silver, lapis
lazuli 8.5×7.8×1.5cm 2007

문화 예술에 관심이 많았던 나는 점차
실생활에서 아름다운 오브제를 신체에
착용하는 일에 심미적 즐거움을 느끼게 되었다. 특정한 공간 내에서 즐기는 회화
등의 예술 작품과 달리, 외양을 아름답게 장식하고 개성을 표현하는 장신구는
마치 자신이 움직이는 조각이 된 듯한 놀라운 경험을 선사했다. 나아가 작가의
작업 의도를 이해하고 작품을 수집하는 과정은 그 자체로 지적인 즐거움이
되었다. 예술의 한 분야로서 장신구가 작가의 내면세계, 자연과의 관계, 사회적
이슈 등의 주제를 밀도 있게 담고 있는 소통의 형태임을 인식하게 된 것이다.
예술장신구는 작가가 세상을 바라보고 사유한 결과물로서 삶에 대한 관점을
다채롭게 만들고, 삶 자체를 풍요롭게 한다. 또한 작업의 개념이나 조형적 요소뿐
아니라, 다양한 재료의 물성을 탐구하고 조합하여, 독창적이고 뛰어난 작품을
만들어내는 장신구 작가들은 마치 연금술사처럼 신선한 자극을 주었다.

컬렉터로서 장신구는 회화 등의 예술 작품에 비해 합리적인 가격으로 수집
가능하다는 점이 매력적이다. 일반 예술 작품에 비해 투자가치는 크지 않으니,
경제적 관점으로는 비효율적일 수 있지만 말이다. 또한 장신구는 크기가 작아
보관할 공간이 그리 넓지 않아도 된다. 하지만 나는 여전히 내게 어울리거나
취향에 맞는 장신구를 사는 소극적인 구매자 수준에 오랫동안 머물렀다. 크기가
아무리 작더라도 수집한 소장품의 수량과 부피가 점차 방대해지면서 개인으로서
보관할 공간의 부족은 현실적 문제로 다가왔다.

한국 현대예술장신구의 수준은 세계적으로 뛰어나다. 하지만 정작 국내에서는
저변이 확대되지 못해, 무한한 가능성을 지닌 미래의 꿈나무들이 작가의 길을
포기하고 생업에 뛰어들어야 하는 것이 안타까운 현실이었다. 이를 바라보며 한

사람의 예술장신구 컬렉터로서 나는 미약하지만, 연속성을 갖고 작가를 발굴하고
후원할 방법에 대해 진지하게 고민하게 되었다. 그 결과 2016년 푸른문화재단을
설립해 작가들을 후원하기 시작했고, 매년 일정 주제를 정해 전시를 기획해
진행하는 단계로 발전하였다. 일련의 전시 기록은 **The Koo Exhibition**이란
다소 말장난 같은 SNS 계정에 아카이빙 되어 있다. 이 명칭은 나의 성 씨인
구와 현대예술장신구에 경도된 **덕후**라는 의미가 중첩된 것으로, 예술 장신구를
열정적으로 즐기는 나의 모습을 반영한 것이다.

사업가로서의 나는 손해가 뻔히 예견되는 일을 벌여서는 안 된다고 생각한다.
한편으로 예술향유자로서의 나는 즐거움과 보람을 위해 일정한 비용을 기꺼이
감수할 수 있지 않을까 생각하여, 공예를 위한 작은 공간을 만들려는 야심 찬
계획까지 세우게 되었다. 초보 컬렉터 시절의 나는 내면의 결핍을 채워가는
과정이 때로 허영과 욕망으로 비칠 수 있다는 사실을 인지하고, 때로는
예술장신구를 열정적으로 구매하는 행위에 다소 불편한 마음이 들기도 했다.
이제는 미술관 소장을 위해 수집한다는 나름의 합리적인 명분을 세우고, 한결
가벼워진 마음으로 소장품의 수량과 범위를 늘려나가고 있다.

컬렉터로서의 길에 들어선 뒤, 컬렉팅에 들이는 시간이 쌓일수록 컬렉션은
개인의 소장을 넘어 예술과 사회를 의식하는 단계로 발전하게 됐다. 나름의
사명감으로 작품을 수집하는 과정에서, 나의 예술장신구 컬렉션은 개인적인
취향과 흥미를 넘어서 일정한 방향성을 갖게 되었다. 컬렉션을 사람들과 공유해,
현대예술장신구에 대한 이해의 확산과 정서적 치유의 기회를 제공하고자 하는
목적이 생긴 것이다. 또한 예술을 전공하는 학생이나 작가들에게 예술적 영감을
불러일으킬 수 있도록 다양한 기법과 개념, 형태의 작업을 시기별로 수집하게
됐다. 예술장신구 분야와 작가의 발전 과정을 기록하겠다는 의지를 품고
아카이브를 구축 중이니, 어찌 보면 개인 컬렉터로서 취향의 일관성은 잃게 된
셈이기도 하다.

작가들은 종종 내가 어떤 기준으로 작품을 구매하는지 궁금해한다. 답은 의외로
간단하다. 일단 내게 심미적으로 즐거움을 주는 작품 또는 개인적으로 의미 있는
작업에 흥미를 갖게 된다. 이러한 감흥은 조화로운 형태, 표현 기법, 색, 재료,
개념 등의 요소로 작품을 분석해 가치를 판단하는 이성적인 인식 과정에서 오는
것은 아니다. 보자마자 직관적으로 끌리고, 마음을 설레게 하는 작업을 선택하는

주관적이고 감성적인 사안에 가깝다. 작가의 영혼이 고스란히 담긴, 손맛이
느껴지는 작업 혹은 실험적이고 창의성이 뛰어난 작업은 그 자체로 감동을 주기
마련이라고 나는 생각한다.

개념적으로 단단한 토대를 구축하고, 조형적으로나 기술적으로도 일정한
아름다움을 갖춘 뛰어난 작품을 만나면 누구라도 이상적인 작업이라고 생각하게
될 것이다. 많은 작품을 보다 보면, 때로 작업 자체에 집중하기보다 난해한
개념만 주장하는 작품을 마주하게 될 때가 있다. 나는 신체에 아름답게 착용하는
장신구의 본질적 기능을 상실하게 되는 작품은 오히려 현학적 허세로 느껴지기도
한다. 이와 반대로 창의성이 느껴지기보다 기법만 뛰어나 손기술에 그쳤다고
생각되는 작업, 본질에서 벗어난 사족과 같은 과도한 장식 등을 만나면 참을 수
없는 가벼움으로 다가온다.

컬렉터로서 성장하며 흥미로운 점은 점차 에너지가 충만한 작업을 선호하게 되고,
착용 시에도 충분히 소화하게 된다는 것이다. 젊은 사람의 손에 가녀린 실반지가
어울린다면, 예술장신구에 익숙한 중장년층은 과감한 큰 반지를 착용할 때 더
잘 어울린다고 느껴진다. 착용하는 사람과 작품이 서로 기운의 조화를 이룰 때
장신구는 효과적으로 그 미감을 드러낸다. 착용자의 마음가짐이나 자신감, 태도에
따라 작품과 사용자 간의 미묘한 상호작용이 마치 신비한 마술처럼 일어나는
것이다. 작은 장신구를 소박하게 착용하기 시작했던 내가, 이제는 가급적 크고,
착용하기 힘들 정도로 과감하고, 다이나믹하며, 독창성을 갖춘, 소위 튀는 작업을
선호하는 컬렉터가 되었으니, 참으로 상전벽해라 아니할 수 없다.

아쉽게도 아직 한국의 예술장신구 시장은 너무 작다. 뛰어난 작가는 많지만,
컬렉터는 찾아보기 힘들다. 미술 시장에서 일정량이 거래되어 작가들이
안정적으로 작품 활동을 할 수 있는 세상은 요원한 듯하다. 대학원 졸업 전시
등에서 과감하고 열정적인 작업을 선보였던 재능 있는 작가가 시장 논리에
의해 판매가 쉬운 상품 위주로 방향을 전환한 것을 보면 안타까움에 가슴이
먹먹해지기도 한다. 한 사람의 컬렉터로서, 나라도 소위 잘 안 팔리는 작품을 사야
한다는 강박관념이 들 정도이다. 한편 작가가 컬렉터로서 나의 의견을 진지하게
받아들이고, 이를 반영하여 작업을 발전시키고, 공모전 등에서 수상해 국제적으로
인정받는 경험을 할 때도 있다. →참고 그림 2 그때의 희열과 보람은 이루 말할 수
없는 것이다. 단순히 구매하고 소장하는 것을 넘어, 작가가 꾸준히 활동할 수

있도록 도울 수 있는 컬렉터가 많이 나오길
바라는 마음이다.

예술적 창의성을 축소된 세계 속에
집약적으로 보여주는 현대미술의 한
분야인 예술장신구는 국내에서는 이제
걸음마를 떼고, 왕성한 청년기로 들어섰다.
장신구가 그저 좋아서 구매하곤 하던
나의 컬렉터로서의 행보도 어느 지점에서
일정한 방향성을 띠게 됐다. 예술장신구를
체계적으로 수집하는 단계로 발전하고,

권슬기 Seulgi Kwon 깊은 밤 Deep in the night
브로치 brooch 실리콘, 안료, 유리 silicone, pigment, glass
18×17×6cm 2014 Art Jewelry Forum Emerging Artist
Award 우승, 미국

나아가 전시 기획자의 길을 걸으며, 나는 삼십여 년에 걸쳐 변모하며 성장해
왔다. 최근에는 즐거움과 보람을 나누기 위해, 사람들이 장신구 컬렉션을 감상할
수 있는 공간을 마련하려는 야심 찬 계획을 세우고 있다. 언젠가 이 공간에
방문할 사람들이, 단순히 개인의 실익을 생각하는 평탄한 길보다, 신나고
재미있는 가시밭길을 택해온 나의 무모함을 이해해 주고, 따스한 눈길로 바라봐
주길 바라는 마음이다. 공간 개장 이후에는 소장품을 도록으로 발간하여,
한국예술장신구 역사를 한눈에 볼 수 있도록 정리하고자 하는 바람이 있다. 이를
통해 장식의 기능을 넘어 한 차원 높은 미술의 영역으로서의 현대예술장신구에
관한 담론과 논의를 확대하는 데 일조하고자 한다.

구혜원은 사업가이자 현대예술장신구 컬렉터로서 지난 30여 년간
장신구를 단순히 수집하는 것을 넘어서 작가와 작업에 대해 의견을
주고받으며 함께 성장해 왔다. 현대예술장신구의 저변 확대를 위해 2016년
푸른문화재단을 설립하여 작가들을 후원하기 시작했고, 나아가 매년
전시를 직접 기획하여 진행하고 있다. 2018년 「사가보월」전부터 2023년
「Just Art」전까지 총 6회 전시에 100여 명의 작가가 참가하였다. 이제는
공예를 위한 공간을 만들어 한국 현대예술장신구의 역사를 담고, 모두가
예술을 향유할 수 있는 장을 만드는 계획을 준비 중이다.

The World of The Koo
The Evolution of a Contemporary Art Jewelry Collector

Haewon Koo

A collector is someone who consistently and systematically gathers and manages objects driven by passion and interest in a particular field. Collecting goes beyond simply acquiring items; it's about building a collection that reflects the collector's taste, discernment, and values. While the spontaneous and emotional satisfaction of collecting is significant, gaining a deeper understanding of an artwork or artist is a core competency of a true collector.

Through collecting, collectors and artists form a symbiotic relationship that transcends the basic roles of owner and creator, establishing a deeply organic connection. For an artist to create meaningful works, a high level of creative activity is essential. By recognizing, evaluating, and purchasing artwork, collectors not only preserve these creations but also provide the impetus for the artist to continue their work. The collector's actions breathe new energy into the artist's life, just as the artist's work enriches the collector's existence. This virtuous cycle allows collectors and artists to mutually influence each other's growth, shape contemporary cultural trends, and co-create art history.

My journey as a collector began with the influence of my elementary school friend, jewelry artist Junghoo Kim. In high school, she surprised us all by announcing her intention to major in art, and after college, she studied abroad. When she returned home in 1989, she won the grand prize in a contemporary art jewelry competition, which led me to visit the Walkerhill Art Museum to congratulate her and see her work. Even though I wasn't well-versed in contemporary art jewelry at the time, the one-of-a-kind pieces were stunning and ignited my latent artistic curiosity. I soon began commissioning art jewelry from her for myself. As a novice collector, I initially found wearing bold art jewelry daunting, so I requested pieces that were small, understated, and simple in design to match my neat suits.

As someone always interested in culture and art, I gradually found aesthetic pleasure in wearing beautiful objects in everyday life. Unlike artworks such as paintings, which are enjoyed in a specific space, jewelry adorns the wearer's appearance and expresses their personality, giving me the extraordinary experience of being a moving sculpture. Furthermore, understanding the artist's intentions and collecting their work has become an intellectual pleasure in itself. I've come to recognize that jewelry, as a form of art, serves as a medium of communication, densely packed with themes such as the artist's inner world, relationships with nature, and social issues. Art jewelry is the result of an artist's reflection on the world, enriching our perspective on life and life itself. Moreover, jewelry artists who explore and combine the physical properties of various materials, alongside their conceptual and formative elements, offer me a fresh and stimulating experience, akin to that of an alchemist's work.
 As a collector, jewelry appeals to me because it's more affordable than paintings or other art objects. On the other hand, it doesn't hold the same investment value as other art forms, making it less efficient from an economic standpoint. Additionally, jewelry's small size means it can be stored in a compact space. Despite this, I've long been a passive buyer, selecting jewelry that suits my taste or complements my style. Yet, as my collection grew, so did the challenge of storage space, a common issue for collectors.

Korean contemporary art jewelry is world-class. However, the field has not expanded significantly in Korea, and it's unfortunate that young talents with immense potential often have to abandon their dreams of becoming professional jewelry artists in favor of more stable careers.

This reality has compelled me, as a collector, to think seriously about how I can continue to discover and support artists. In 2016, I founded the Pureun Culture Foundation to support jewelry artists, and it has since evolved into an initiative where I organize exhibitions with specific themes each year. These exhibitions are documented on a social media account called **The Koo Exhibition**. The name **The Koo** has a dual meaning: **Koo** refers to my surname, and it also playfully resembles the Korean slang **deokhu** which describes someone who is intensely passionate or a **geek** about something, reflecting my deep passion for art jewelry.

As a businesswoman, I usually avoid ventures that I know will result in financial loss. However, as an art lover, I'm willing to invest in the pleasure and reward that art brings, which led me to make ambitious plans to create a small museum space dedicated to crafts. Early in my collecting career, I recognized that the process of filling an inner deficiency can sometimes come across as vanity and greed, and I sometimes felt uncomfortable with the act of enthusiastically purchasing art jewelry. Now, with the rationale of collecting for the museum, I'm growing the number and scope of my collection with a lighter heart.

Once on the path of a collector, as time spent collecting accumulated, my collection evolved from mere personal acquisition to a stage of contemplating art and society. With a sense of mission, my art jewelry collection developed a direction beyond personal taste, with the purpose of sharing the collection to promote understanding of contemporary art jewelry and provide opportunities for emotional healing. Additionally, I began collecting jewelry of various techniques, concepts, and forms by season to inspire artists and students. With the intent to document the development of art jewelry and its creators, I'm in the process of building an archive, which may mean losing the consistency of personal taste as a collector.

Jewelry artists often ask about the criteria I use when purchasing artworks. The answer is surprisingly simple. I'm initially drawn to works that give me aesthetic pleasure or hold personal significance. This appreciation doesn't arise from a rational analysis of harmonious forms, expressive techniques, colors, materials, or concepts. Instead, it's a subjective and emotional response, where I'm intuitively attracted to pieces that captivate me and stir my emotions. I believe that works imbued with the artist's soul, evident craftsmanship, or those that are experimental and exceptionally creative, possess the power to move me.

While conceptually robust works with a certain aesthetic or technical beauty are ideal, some pieces focus more on obscure concepts than on the artwork itself. Such jewelry can sometimes feel like pretentious displays of erudition, rather than meaningful art. Conversely, works that excel only in technique without evoking creativity or those burdened with excessive decoration can feel superficial.

As I've grown as a collector, I've come to prefer jewelry that is full of energy, and I've learned to wear it in a way that allows me to fully embrace it. A thin ring may suit a young hand, but the boldness of a large ring feels more fitting when worn by someone experienced with art jewelry in their later years. When the wearer and the artwork harmonize, the jewelry reveals its beauty. Depending on the wearer's mindset, confidence, and attitude, a subtle interaction between the artwork and the user occurs, almost like a mysterious magic. From starting with small, modest pieces, I've evolved into a collector who favors bold, dynamic, and creative jewelry that stands out, reflecting how much my tastes have changed.

Unfortunately, the art jewelry market in Korea remains small. While there are many talented artists, it is challenging for collectors to find them.
A world where art jewelry is consistently traded and artists can engage in stable creative activities seem distant. It is disheartening to see talented artists who showcased their work passionately in graduate exhibitions shift towards more commercial products due to market pressures. As a collector, I sometimes feel an obsession to buy art jewelry that is not commonly sold. Yet, there are moments when artists take my opinions seriously, incorporate them into their work, and experience the thrill and satisfaction of winning international recognition. Therefore, beyond just buying and owning, I hope to see more collectors emerge who can support artists in their ongoing activities, enabling them to thrive.

Art jewelry, a field of contemporary art that intensively showcases creativity in a **miniaturized world**, is now taking its first steps and entering its vigorous youth in Korea. As a collector who once purchased jewelry simply out of personal preference, my journey has led to a more systematic approach to collecting and eventually to curating exhibitions. Over the past thirty years, I have grown and transformed, and I am now ambitiously planning to create a space where people can appreciate jewelry collections. I hope that visitors to this space will understand my audacity in choosing a challenging yet exciting path, not simply seeking personal gain, and will view it with warm regard. After the space opens, I aspire to publish a catalog documenting the history of Korean art jewelry, aiming to expand the discourse on contemporary art jewelry beyond its decorative function into a higher realm of art.

Haewon Koo is a businesswoman and collector of contemporary jewelry who has grown over the past 30 years by not only collecting jewelry but also interacting with jewelry artists.
To promote contemporary jewelry, Pureun Culture Foundation was established in 2016 to support artists and organize annual exhibitions. From 「SAGABOWOL」 in 2018 to 「Just Art」 in 2023, about 100 artists have participated in six exhibitions. Currently, she is preparing a plan to create a space for crafts, documenting the history of Korean contemporary jewelry and creating a place where everyone can enjoy art.

작가 약력
ARTIST BIOGRAPHY

강미나 Mina Kang

김경진 Kyungjin Kim

김민정 Minjeong Kim

김수진 Sujin Kim

김아랑 Arang Kim

김유정 Yoojung Kim

김지민 Jimin Kim

김한나 Hanna Kim

김혜원 Hyewon Kim

김희앙 Hee-ang Kim

노은주 Eunjoo Noh

민준석 Junsuk Min

박영빈 Youngbin Park

백시내 Sinae Baik

서예슬 Yeseul Seo

서은영 Eunyoung Seo

성코코 Coco Sung

송유경 Yookyung Song

심진아 Jina Sim

양지원 Jiwon Yang

엄민재 Min-jae Eom

엄세희 Sehee Um

엄유진 Youjin Um

원재선 Jaesun Won

유다흰 Dahin Yoo

유아미 Ahmi Yu

윤지예 Jiye Yun

이나진 Najin Lee

이남경 Namkyung Lee

이선용 Seonyong Lee

이소리 Sohri Yi

이승열 Sungyeoul Lee

이영주 Youngjoo Lee

이재현 Jaehyun Lee

이주현 Joohyun Lee

이진경 Jinkyung Lee

이형찬 Hyungchan Lee

임제운 Jewoon Lim

임종석 Jongseok Lim

장지영 Jiyoung Jang

조완희 Wanhee Cho

진유리 Yuri Jin

최예진 Ye-jin Choi

최윤정 Yoonjung Choi

최혜영 Hyeyoung Choi

한은석 Eunseok Han

한은지 Eunji Han

한주희 Joohee Han

현성환 Seong-hwan Hyun

홍예인 Yein Hong

강미나 Mina Kang (1987–) →26

학력
2013 국민대학교 대학원 졸업, 서울 | 2010 경기대학교 졸업, 수원
개인전
2016 모놀로그, 갤러리 썸머, 세종 | 2015 나날, 핸더스 갤러리, 서울
단체전
2024 장식 너머 발언, 서울공예박물관, 서울 | 2021 사물을 대하는 태도, 팔라조리따, 이탈리아 밀라노 | 2019 생활미학, 메트로폴리탄미술관, 필리핀 마닐라 | 2018 컬렉트, 사치 갤러리, 영국 런던 | 2017 Révélations, 그랑팔레, 프랑스 파리
소장·수상·주요활동
서울공예박물관, 서울 | 2013 특선, Preziosa Young, 이탈리아 | 2012 1등상, BKV-Prize, 독일
현재
장신구 작가
금속공방 스튜디오 엠 대표
kmn1106@naver.com
@minakang__

Education
2013 M.F.A. Kookmin University, Seoul Korea | 2012 B.F.A. Kyonggi University, Suwon Korea
Solo Exhibitions
2016 Monologue, Gallery Summer, Sejong Korea | 2015 Days, Handus Gallery, Seoul Korea
Group Exhibitions
2024 Beyond Adornment, SeMoCA, Seoul Korea | 2021 All About Attitude, Palazzo Litta, Milano Italy | 2019 Korean Life Aesthetics, Metropolitan Museum, Manila Philippines | 2018 COLLECT, Saatchi Gallery, London UK | 2017 Révélations, Grand Palais, Paris France
Collections·Awards·Activities
SeMoCA, Korea | 2013 Special Mention, Preziosa Young, Italy | 2012 1st Prize, BKV-Prize, Germany
Present
Jewelry Artist, Director of Studio M
kmn1106@naver.com
@minakang__

김경진 Kyungjin Kim (1983–) →20

학력
2019 뉘른베르크 조형예술대학 졸업, 독일 뉘른베르크 | 2006 경기대학교 졸업, 수원
개인전
2022 쓰이지만 쓰이지 않는, 예술의전당 한가람디자인미술관, 서울
단체전
2022 해후, KCDF 갤러리, 서울 | 2022 Wall Project Visible Side, 킵인터치, 서울 | 2021 공예트렌트페어-O&O, 코엑스, 서울 | 2021 PAPIER, 밤베르크 미술협회, 독일 밤베르크
소장·수상·주요활동
푸른문화재단, 서울 | 2019 마쩨 졸업작품상, 갤러리 마쩨, 네덜란드 | 2018 1등상, 일루션 레그니차 국제주얼리공모전, 폴란드 | 2017 입선, 탈렌테, 독일
현재
장신구 작가
rudwls2004@naver.com
www.kyungjinkim.com

Education
2019 Dpl. Akademie der Bildende Künste Nürnberg, Nürnberg Germany | 2006 B.F.A. Kyonggi University, Suwon Korea
Solo Exhibitions
2022 Used but not used, SAC, Seoul Korea
Group Exhibitions
2022 Reunion, KCDF Gallery, Seoul Korea | 2022 Wall Project Visible Side, Keep in touch, Seoul Korea
2021 Craft Trend Fair-O&O, COEX, Seoul Korea | 2021 PAPIER, Kunstverein, Bamberg Germany
Collections·Awards·Activities
Pureun Cultural Foundation, Korea | 2019 Marzee Graduate Prize, Galerie Marzee, Nederlands | 2018 1st Grand Prize, ILLUSION Legnica Int. Jewellery Competition, Poland | 2017 Selected, TALENTE, Germany
Present
Jewelry Artist
rudwls2004@naver.com, www.kyungjinkim.com

김민정 Minjeong Kim (1982–) →48

학력
2009 서울대학교 대학원 졸업, 서울
단체전
2020 짝, 산울림 아트앤크래프트, 서울 | 2017 풀고 또 이음, 산울림 아트앤크래프트, 서울 | 2015 SN2015:01_10, 갤러리 아원, 서울 | 2013 Gift·ed, 마노 컨템포러리 주얼리앤오브젝트, 대만 타이베이 | 2013 Au pays du matin calme, 라뜰리에, 프랑스 파리
소장·수상·주요활동
2008 입선, NTJ | 국제주얼리디자인공모전, 네덜란드
현재
장신구 작가
kimminjeong.39719@gmail.com

Education
2009 M.F.A. Seoul National University, Seoul Korea
Group Exhibitions
2020 The other one earring, Sanwoollim Art&Craft, Seoul Korea | 2017 Unhook and Connect, Sanwoollim Art&Craft, Seoul Korea | 2015 SN2015:01_10, Gallery Ahwon, Seoul Korea | 2013 Gift·ed, MANO Contemporary Jewellery&Object, Taipei Taiwan | 2013 Au pays du matin calme, L'Atelier, Paris France
Collections·Awards·Activities
2008 Selected, NTJ 2008, Netherlands
Present
Jewelry Artist
kimminjeong.39719@gmail.com

김수진 Sujin Kim (1993–) →28

학력
2021 힐데스하임 조형대학 졸업, 독일 힐데스하임 | 2017 홍익대학교 졸업, 서울
개인전
2023 The Moment, 갤러리 아원, 서울
단체전
2024 소망을 위한 움직임, SASS 갤러리, 서울 | 2023 낯선 슴, 남산골 한옥마을, 서울 | 2023 Objet Objet Objet, 오브젝티브 스튜디오, 서울 2023 금속과 장신구, 갤러리 마쩨, 네덜란드 네이메헌 | 2022 ASIA MON AMOUR, 72 Warren Street, 미국 뉴욕
소장·수상·주요활동
2022 1등상, BKV-Prize, 독일 | 2021 마쩨 졸업작품상, 갤러리 마쩨, 네덜란드
현재
장신구 및 오브제 작가
tn2568@gmail.com

@sujin_kim_in

Education
2021 M.F.A. FH Hildesheim für Gestaltung, Hildesheim Germany | 2017 B.F.A. Hongik University, Seoul Korea
Solo Exhibitions
2023 The Moment, Gallery Ahwon, Seoul Korea
Group Exhibitions
2024 Movement for Wishes, Gallery SASS, Seoul Korea | 2023 Unfamiliar Combination, Namsangol Hanok Village, Seoul Korea | 2023 Objet Objet Objet, Objective Studio, Seoul Korea | 2023 Metal and Jewellery, Galerie Marzee, Nijmegen Netherlands | 2022 ASIA MON AMOUR, 72 Warren Street, NYC USA
Collections·Awards·Activities
2022 1st Prize, BKV-Prize, Germany
2021 Marzee Graduate Prize, Galerie Marzee, Nederlands
Present
Jewelry and Object Artist
tn2568@gmail.co
@sujin_kim_in

김아랑 Arang Kim (1981–) →42

학력
2015 국민대학교 대학원 졸업, 서울
개인전
2019 환상 박물관, 갤러리 담, 서울 | 2019 환상 이야기, KCDF 윈도우 갤러리, 서울
단체전
2022 Ars Longa, 갤러리 SP, 서울 | 2020 뉴 타이베이 시티 국제금속공예공모전, 황금박물관, 대만 타이베이 | 2019 LOOT MAD, 아트앤디자인박물관, 미국 뉴욕
소장·수상·주요활동
2020 우수상, 뉴 타이베이 시티 국제금속공예공모전, 대만 | 2017 금상, 제17회 국제주얼리디자인공모전, 서울 | 2013 입선, BKV-Prize, 독일
현재
장신구 작가
darkchild01@naver.com

Education
M.F.A. Kookmin University, Seoul Korea
Solo Exhibitions
2019 Evoke Fantasy, Gallery Dam, Seoul Korea | 2019 Fantasy Story, KCDF Window Gallery, Seoul Korea

Group Exhibitions
2022 Ars Longa, Gallery SP, Seoul Korea | 2020 New Taipei City Int. Metal Crafts Competition Winners Exhibition, Gold Museum, Taipei Taiwan | 2019 LOOT MAD, Museum of Arts and Design, NYC USA
Collections·Awards·Activities
2020 Merit Award, New Taipei City Int. Metal Crafts Competition, Taiwan | 2017 Gold Prize, 17th Int. Jewelry Design Competition, Korea
2013 Selected, BKV-Prize, Germany
Present
Jewelry Artist
darkchild01@naver.com

김유정 Yoojung Kim (1991–) →36

학력
2024 서울대학교 박사 수료, 서울 | 2020 영국왕립예술학교 대학원 졸업, 영국 런던 | 2018 서울대학교 대학원 졸업, 서울 | 2015 서울대학교 졸업, 서울
개인전
2020 The Moment Series, 스페이스 금채, 서울
단체전
2024 Treasure Peninsula, 수퍼+센터코트, 독일 뮌헨 | 2023 MAD About Jewelry, 아트앤디자인박물관, 미국 뉴욕 | 2022 Ars Longa, 갤러리 SP, 서울 | 2021 수집으로부터, Wang&Buck 갤러리, 덴마크 코펜하겐 | 2021 URL/IRL Exhibition, 갤러리 SO, 영국 런던
소장·수상·주요활동
국립장식예술박물관, 노르웨이 | 푸른문화재단, 서울 | 2024 입선, 슈묵, 독일 | 2023 입선, 이타미 | 국제공예공모전, 일본 | 2023 입선, 탈렌테, 독일 | 2022 입선, ENJOIA'T 어워드, 스페인 | 2019 학생 1등상, 베니스 디자인위크장신구공모전, 이탈리아
현재
장신구 작가, 서울대학교 출강
yoojungkimstudio@gmail.com
www.yoojungkim.com
@yoojungkim_studio

Education
2024 D.F.A. Candidate, Seoul National University, Seoul Korea | 2020 M.A. Royal College of Art, London UK |

2018 M.F.A. Seoul National University, Seoul Korea | 2015 B.F.A. Seoul National University, Seoul Korea
Solo Exhibitions
2020 The Moment Series, Space Geumchae, Seoul Korea
Group Exhibitions
2024 Treasure Peninsula, Super+Centercourt, Munich Germany | 2023 MAD About Jewelry, Museum of Arts and Design, NYC USA
2022 Ars Longa, Gallery SP, Seoul Korea | 2021 From Collect, Wang&Buck Gallery, Copenhagen Denmark | 2021 URL/IRL Exhibition, Gallery SO, London UK
Collections·Awards·Activities
National Museum of Decorative Arts, Norway | Pureun Cultural Foundation, Korea | 2024 Selected, SCHMUCK, Germany | 2023 Selected, ITAMI Int. Craft Competition, Japan | 2023 Selected, TALENTE, Germany | 2022 Selected, ENJOIA'T Awards, Spain | 2019 1st Student Prize, Venice Design Week Jewelry Selection, Italy
Present
Jewelry Artist, Lecturer at Seoul National University, Seoul Korea
yoojungkimstudio@gmail.com
www.yoojungkim.com
@yoojungkim_studio

김지민 Jimin Kim (1983–) →38

학력
2010 국민대학교 대학원 졸업, 서울 | 2007 국민대학교 졸업, 서울
개인전
2013 서랍 속 이야기, 더 브릿지, 서울 | 2010 기록:Recorded, 소노팩토리, 서울
단체전
2023 가로지르다, 갤러리 마쩨, 네덜란드 네이메헌 | 2021 귀걸이, 과거와 현재를 꿰다, 서울공예박물관, 서울 | 2021 No attachment, Paperwork Glockenbach, 독일 뮌헨 | 2017 Light Weight, KONSTHANTVERKARNA, 스웨덴 스톡홀름 | 2017 Back both Future in South Korea, 갤러리 라, 네덜란드 암스테르담 | 2015 Révélations, 그랑팔레, 프랑스 파리
소장·수상·주요활동
Die Neue Sammlung,

디자인미술관, 독일
현재
장신구 작가
arty.jimin@gmail.com
@jiminkim_artjewellery

Education
2010 M.F.A. Kookmin University, Seoul Korea | 2007 B.F.A. Kookmin University, Seoul Korea
Solo Exhibitions
2013 Memories in drawer, THE BRIDGE Gallery, Seoul Korea | 2010 Recorded, SONO FACTORY, Seoul Korea
Group Exhibitions
2023 TRAVERSE, Galerie Marzee, Nijmegen Netherlands | 2021 Earring, Connecting the past and Present, SeMoCA, Seoul Korea | 2021 No attachment, Paperwork Glockenbach, Munich Germany | 2017 Light Weight, KONSTHANTVERKARNA, Stockholm Sweden
2017 Back both Future in South Korea, Galerie Ra, Amsterdam Netherlands
2015 Révélations, Grand Palais, Paris France
Collections·Awards·Activities
Die Neue Sammlung, The Design Museum, Germany
Present
Jewelry Artist
arty.jimin@gmail.com,
@jiminkim_artjewellery

김한나 Hanna Kim (1986–) →114

학력
2013 국민대학교 대학원 졸업, 서울 | 2010 국민대학교 졸업, 서울
개인전
2020 공예트랜드페어, 코엑스, 서울
단체전
2024 Wearing RED, 파티나 갤러리, 미국 샌타페이 | 2023 가로지르다, 갤러리 마쩨, 네덜란드 네이메헌 | 2022 Ars Longa, 갤러리 SP, 서울 | 2021 HO!HO!HO!, 갤러리 Friends of Carlotta, 스위스 취리히 | 2018 키네시스-몸과 장식, 공근혜 갤러리, 서울 | 2017 오너먼테이션, 유리지공예관, 서울 | 2013 욕망하는 꽃, 갤러리 아트링크, 서울
소장·수상·주요활동
푸른문화재단, 서울 | 서울특별시 박물관과, 서울 | 2021 입선, 탈렌테, 독일 | 2009 퍼처스 어워드, 36th

Annual Toys Designed by Artists, 미국
현재
장신구 작가
hannale0@naver.com
@hannale0

Education
2013 M.F.A. Kookmin University, Seoul Korea | 2010 B.F.A. Kookmin University, Seoul Korea
Solo Exhibitions
2020 Craft Trend Fair, COEX, Seoul Korea
Group Exhibitions
2024 Wearing RED, Patina Gallery, Santa Fe USA | 2023 TRAVERSE, Galerie Marzee, Nijmegen Netherlands | 2022 Ars Longa, Gallery SP, Seoul Korea | 2021 HO!HO!HO!, Gallery Friends of Carlotta, Zurich Switzerland | 2018 Kinesis-Body and Ornament, Gallery KONG, Seoul Korea 2017 Ornamentation, Yoolizzy Craft Museum, Seoul Korea | 2023 Flower of Desire, Gallery Artlink, Seoul Korea
Collections·Awards·Activities
Pureun Cultural Foundation, Korea
Korea Seoul City Museum, Korea
2021 Selected, TALENTE, Germany
2009 Purchase Award, 36th Toys Designed by Artists, USA
Present
Jewelry Artist
hannale0@naver.com,
@hannale0

김혜원 Hyewon Kim (1980–) →44

학력
2007 국민대학교 대학원 졸업, 서울 | 2004 동덕여자대학교 졸업, 서울
개인전
2011 페르소나, 갤러리 담, 서울
단체전
2023 가로지르다, 갤러리 마쩨, 네덜란드 네이메헌 | 2018 사가보월, 이유진 갤러리, 서울 | 2013 Unexpected Pleasures, 디자인미술관, 영국 런던
소장·수상·주요활동
디자인미술관, 영국
현재
장신구 작가
kimhyewon80@naver.com

Education
2007 M.F.A. Kookmin University, Seoul Korea | 2003 B.F.A. Dongduk Women's University, Seoul Korea
Solo Exhibitions
2011 Persona, Gallery Dam, Seoul Korea
Group Exhibitions
2023 TRAVERSE, Galerie Marzee, Nijmegen Netherlands | 2018 SAGABOWOL, Lee Eugean Gallery, Seoul Korea | 2013 Unexpected Pleasures, The Design Museum, London UK
Collections · Awards · Activities
The Design Museum, UK
Present
Jewelry Artist
kimhyewon80@naver.com

김희앙 Hee-ang Kim (1989–) →68

학력
2015 국민대학교 대학원 졸업, 서울 | 2012 국민대학교 졸업, 서울
개인전
2024 Beyond dining table, 클로저 갤러리, 중국 베이징 | 2024 피어나는 시간, 가온 갤러리, 서울 | 2021 매일의 도약, 학고재 아트센터, 서울 | 2018 포착된 순간, 갤러리 아원, 서울
단체전
2024 장식 너머 발언, 서울공예박물관, 서울 | 2023 Wild Herbs, Chance, and Seeds of Desire, 바이스벌사, 스위스 로잔 | 2023 가로지르다, 갤러리 마쩨, 네덜란드 네이메헌
소장 · 수상 · 주요활동
Die Neue Sammlung, 디자인미술관, 독일 | 서울공예박물관, 서울 | 푸른문화재단, 서울 | 2015 우수상, 뉴 타이베이 시티 국제금속공예공모전, 대만 | 2023 폴리머 워크 워크숍 강의, 체코 | 2017 V&A-KCDF 교류협력 워크숍 선정, 영국
현재
장신구 작가
siculala@naver.com,
www.heeang.com,
@heeang_kim

Education
2015 M.F.A. Kookmin University, Seoul Korea | 2012 B.F.A. Kookmin University, Seoul Korea
Solo Exhibitions
2024 Beyond dining table, Closer Gallery, Beijing China | 2024 Time to bloom, Gaon Gallery, Seoul Korea | 2021 Leap of everyday, Hakgojae Art Center, Seoul Korea | 2018 Captured moments, Gallery Ahwon, Seoul Korea
Group Exhibitions
2024 Beyond Adornment, SeMoCA, Seoul Korea | 2023 Wild Herbs, Chance, and Seeds of Desire, Viceversa, Lausanne Switzerland | 2023 TRAVERSE, Galerie Marzee, Nijmegen Netherlands
Collections · Awards · Activities
Die Neue Sammlung, The Design Museum, Germany | SeMoCA, Korea | Pureun Cultural Foundation, Korea | 2015 Quality Award, New Taipei City Int. Metal Crafts Competition, Taiwan | 2023 Polymer Week Workshop, Czech | 2017 V&A-KCDF Int. Maker's Workshop, UK
Present
Jewelry Artist
siculala@naver.com,
www.heeang.com,
@heeang_kim

노은주 Eunjoo Noh (1978–) →66

학력
2004 국민대학교 대학원 졸업, 서울 | 2001 건국대학교 졸업, 충주
개인전
2022 두 개의 브로치, 갤러리 오, 서울 | 2011 ROOF, 크래프트 아원, 서울 | 2006 노은주 금속공예전, 가나아트 스페이스, 서울
단체전
2023 청서둠, 갤러리 엘, 서울 | 2018 사가보월전, 이유진 갤러리, 서울 | 2015 Take Away koru-jewelry, 갤러리 조한S, 핀란드 헬싱키 | 2013 FEINGE, 갤러리 유비, 중국 베이징 | 2008 食과 工-또 다른 네버엔딩스토리, 치우금속공예관, 서울
소장 · 수상 · 주요활동
푸른문화재단, 서울 | 2008 입선, 탈렌테, 독일 | 2002 입선, 이타미 국제공예공모전, 일본 | 2008 수록, Ardon New Jewellery, 아만다 맨슬, 영국 | 2008 수록, The Compendium Finale of Contemporary Jewellers, 달링, 독일

현재
장신구 작가
nonjoo97@gmail.com
@eun.joo.noh

Education
2004 M.F.A. Kookmin University, Seoul Korea | 2001 B.F.A. Konkuk University, Chungju Korea
Solo Exhibitions
2022 Two Ornaments for Brooch, Gallery O, Seoul Korea | 2011 ROOF, Craft Ahwon, Seoul Korea | 2006 Metal Craft By Eunjoo Noh, Gana Art Space, Seoul Korea
Group Exhibitions
2023 Chung Seo Doom, Gallery EL, Seoul Korea | 2018 Sagabowol, Lee Eugean Gallery, Seoul Korea | 2015 Take Away koru-jewelry, Galleria johan S, Helsinki Finland | 2013 FEINGE, Gallery Ubi, Beijing China | 2008 Foods and crafts-another never ending story, Chiwoo Craft Museum, Seoul Korea
Collections · Awards · Activities
Pureun Cultural Foundation, Korea | 2008 Selected, TALENTE, Germany | 2002 Selected, ITAMI Int. Craft Competition, Japan | 2008 Featured, Ardon New Jewellery, Amanda Mansell, UK | 2008 Featured, The Compendium Finale of Contemporary Jewellers, Darling, Garmany
Present
Jewelry Artist
nonjoo97@gmail.com
@eun.joo.noh

민준석 Junsuk Min (1973–) →108

학력
2008 로체스터 공과대학 대학원 졸업, 미국 로체스터 | 2001 서울대학교 대학원 졸업, 서울 | 1998 서울대학교 졸업, 서울 |
개인전
2018 Rolling Circles the 2nd, 갤러리 아원, 서울 | 2016 Rotating Circles, 갤러리 담, 서울 | 2014 Circulating Circles, 갤러리 보고재, 서울 | 2012 유희적 움직임, 캘빈 갤러리, 미국 그랜드 래피즈 외 5회
단체전
2024 장식 너머 발언, 서울공예박물관, 서울 | 2023 크래프토이 파크, 갤러리 아원, 서울 | 2022 Ars Longa, 갤러리 SP, 서울 | 2022 Chrono Object the 2nd, KCDF 갤러리, 서울 | 2021 연리지 둘이서 하나이 되어, 아름지기, 서울
소장 · 수상 · 주요활동
푸른문화재단, 서울 | 2003 특선, 청주국제공예 비엔날레, 청주 | 2019-2023 전시기획, 크래프토이, 서울 | 2022 전시기획, Chrono Object the 2nd, 서울
현재
장신구 작가, 금속공예가, Team Craftoy 대표
junsuk10@naver.com, @junsuk11

Education
2008 M.F.A. Rochester Institute of Technology, Rochester USA | 2001 M.F.A. Seoul National University, Seoul Korea | 1998 B.F.A. Seoul National University, Seoul Korea
Solo Exhibitions
2018 Rolling Circles the 2nd, Gallery Ahwon, Seoul Korea | 2016 Rotating Circles, Gallery Dam, Seoul Korea | 2014 Circulating Circles, Gallery Vogoze, Seoul Korea | 2012 Enjoyable Movements, Calvin Gallery, Grand Rapids USA and 5 times
Group Exhibitions
2024 Beyond Adorment, SeMoCA, Seoul Korea | 2023 Craftoy Park, Gallery Ahwon, Seoul Korea | 2022 Ars Longa, Gallery SP, Seoul Korea | 2022 Chrono Object the 2nd, KCDF Gallery, Seoul Korea | 2021 Yeonliji Two Becoming One, Arumjigi, Seoul Korea
Collections · Awards · Activities
Pureun Cultural Foundation, Korea | 2003 Special Selected, Cheongju Int. Craft Competition, Korea | 2019-2023 Curated, Craftoy, Korea | 2022 Curated, Chrono Objects the 2nd, Korea
Present
Jewelry Artist, Metal Artist, RePresentative of Team Craftoy
junsuk10@naver.com, @junsuk11

박영빈 Youngbin Park (1982–) →118

학력
2010 서울대학교 대학원 졸업, 서울 | 2009 알키미아 졸업, 이탈리아 피렌체 | 2005 동덕여자대학교 졸업, 서울

개인전
2010 미로, 갤러리 담, 서울
단체전
2023 빈손, 갤러리 1898, 서울 |
2021 블루 불확실한 봄, 갤러리 바움,
파주 | 2017 풀고 또 이음, 산울림
아트앤크래프트, 서울 | 2009 SOFA
시카고, 샤론 크란센 아트, 미국
시카고 | 2009 마쩨 국제졸업작품전,
갤러리 마쩨, 네덜란드 네이메헌
소장·수상·주요활동
푸른문화재단, 서울
현재
장신구 작가, 아멜리아 주얼리 대표
bin9326@gmail.com,
@ameliajewelry_

Education
2010 M.F.A. Seoul National
University, Seoul Korea | 2009
Dpl. Alchimia, Florence Italy |
2005 B.F.A. Dongduk Women's
University, Seoul Korea
Solo Exhibitions
2010 me路, Gallery Dam, Seoul
Korea
Group Exhibitions
2023 Empty hands, Gallery
1898, Seoul Korea | 2021
Blue Uncertain Spring, Gallery
Baum, Paju Korea | 2017 Unhook
and Connect, Sanwoolim
Art&craft, Seoul Korea | 2009
SOFA Chicago, Charon Kranson
Art, Chicago USA | 2009
Marzee Int. Graduate Show,
Galerie Marzee, Nijmegen
Netherlands
Collections·Awards·Activities
Pureun Cultural Foundation,
Korea
Present
Jewelry Artist, Director of
Amelia Jewelry
bin9326@gmail.com,
@ameliajewelry_

백시내 Sinae Baik (1990–)   →46

학력
2017 국민대학교
테크노디자인전문대학원 졸업, 서울
개인전
2023 그래서 여기에 있다, 마루누마
예술의 숲, 일본
단체전
2023 청년미술상점, 예술의전당
한가람미술관, 서울 | 2022 One
and More 신당창작아케이드,
신세계 L&B, 코사이어티
서울숲, 서울 | 2021 JOYA
아트주얼리&오브젝트,

디자인박물관, 스페인 바르셀로나 |
2021 루마니아 주얼리위크, 루마니아
부쿠레슈티 | 2020 Friedrich
Becker Prize, Deutsches
Goldschmiedehaus, 독일 하나우
소장·수상·주요활동
2022 수록, 한눈에 보는 칠보, 서울 |
2019 우승, Autor Media Award,
포르투갈 | 2017 입선, 이타미
국제공예공모전, 일본
현재
장신구 작가
baiksn0308@naver.com,
www.sinaebaik.com

Education
2017 M.D.A. Kookmin University,
Seoul Korea
Solo Exhibitions
2023 Therefore I Am, Marunuma
Art Park, Japan
Group Exhibitions
2023 Young Artist's Shop, SAC,
Seoul Korea | 2022 One and
More, Seoul Art Space_Sindang,
Shinsegae L&B, Cociety,
Seoul Korea | 2021 JOYA Art
Jewellery&Objects Fair, Museu
del Disseny, Barcelona Spain
| 2021 Romanian Jewelry
Week, Bucharest Romania |
2020 Friedrich Becker Prize,
Deutsches Goldschmiedehaus,
Hanau Germany
Collections·Awards·Activities
2022 Featured, 'Chilbo' Korea
Craft & Design Resource Book,
Korea | 2019 Winner, Autor
Media Award, Portugal | 2017
Selected, ITAMI Int. Craft
Competition, Japan
Present
Jewelry Artist
baiksn0308@naver.com,
www.sinaebaik.com

서예슬 Yeseul Seo (1986–)   →64

학력
2013 국민대학교 대학원 졸업, 서울 |
2010 국민대학교 졸업, 서울
개인전
2021 어울림 정원, 김현주 갤러리,
서울 | 2018 연결된 삶, 갤러리 아원,
서울
단체전
2024 장식 너머 발언,
서울공예박물관, 서울 | 2023
가로지르다, 갤러리 마쩨, 네덜란드
네이메헌 | 2023 배치 그리고 생성,
갤러리 마크, 서울 | 2022 Ars
Longa, 갤러리 SP, 서울 | 2022

이어가기, 서울시립미술관 창고, 서울
| 2021 블루 불확실한 봄, 갤러리
바움, 파주 | 2017 Koreanisch,
바이에른 미술공예협회, 독일 뮌헨
소장·수상·주요활동
2010 퍼처스 어워드, 37th Annual
Toys Designed by Artists, 미국 |
2009 퍼처스 어워드, 36th Annual
Toys Designed by Artists, 미국
현재
공예 작가, 대구가톨릭대학교 출강
silbia0204@naver.com,
@be_melted

Education
2013 M.F.A. Kookmin University,
Seoul Korea | 2010 B.F.A.
Kookmin University, Seoul
Korea
Solo Exhibitions
2021 Mingling garden, KHJ
Gallery, Seoul Korea | 2018 The
connected life, Gallery Ahwon,
Seoul Korea
Group Exhibitions
2024 BEYOND ADORNMENT,
SeMoCA, Seoul Korea | 2023
TRAVERSE, Gallery Marzee,
Nijmegen Netherlands | 2023
Arrangement&Becoming,
Gallery Mark, Seoul Korea |
2022 Ars Longa, Gallery SP,
Seoul Korea | 2022 Dot to
dot, SeMA, Seoul Korea | 2021
Blue An Uncertain Spring,
Gallery Baum, Paju Korea |
2017 Koreanisch, Bayerischer
kunstgewerbeverein, Munich
Germany
Collections·Awards·Activities
2010 Purchase Award, 37th
Annual Toys Designed by
Artists, USA | 2009 Purchase
Award, 36th Annual Toys
Designed by Artists, USA
Present
Craft Artist, Lecturer at Daegu
Catholic University, Gyeongsan
Korea
silbia0204@naver.com,
@be_melted

서은영 Eunyoung Seo (1994–)
→96

학력
2021 성신여자대학교 대학원 졸업,
서울 | 2017 성신여자대학교 졸업,
서울
개인전
2022 흔적, 예올, 서울
단체전
2023 정원산책, 갤러리 완물, 서울
| 2020 장식하다, 예올, 서울 |

2020 사월의 장식, 통인화랑, 서울
| 2019 Enjoia't, 디자인미술관,
스페인 바르셀로나 | 2018
연희아트페어, 보스토크, 서울 | 2018
케이크 포크 토크, 문화공간 숨도,
서울
소장·수상·주요활동
2019 입선, Enjoia't 어워드, 스페인
현재
장신구 및 공예 작가
eaddj@naver.com, @eaddj

Education
2021 M.F.A. Sungshin University,
Seoul Korea | 2017 B.F.A.
Sungshin Women's University,
Seoul Korea
Solo Exhibitions
2022 Trace, YÉOL, Seoul Korea
Group Exhibitions
2023 Walk in the garden,
Gallery Wannmul, Seoul Korea
| 2020 Ornament, YÉOL, Seoul
Korea | 2020 April Ornament,
Tong In Gallery, Seoul Korea
| 2019 Enjoia't, Museu del
Disseny, Barcelona Spain | 2018
Yeonhui Art Fair, Vostok, Seoul
Korea | 2018 Cake Talk Fork,
soomdo, Seoul Korea
Collections·Awards·Activities
2019 Selected, Enjoia't Awards,
Spain
Present
Jewelry and Craft Artist
eaddj@naver.com, @eaddj

성코코 Coco Sung (1979–)   →140

학력
2014 부르크 기비헨슈타인 미술대학
할레 졸업, 독일 할레 | 2002
울산대학교 졸업, 울산
개인전
2019 갤러리 포, 스웨덴 예테보리
| 2018 갤러리 라온, 울산 | 2017
갤러리 비로, 독일 뮌헨
단체전
2024 장식 너머 발언,
서울공예박물관, 서울 | 2022
Ars Longa, 갤러리 SP, 서울
| 2021 TWOxTWO for AIDS
and Art, 댈러스미술관, 미국
댈러스 | 2021 Frauen März,
템펠호프쇤베르크박물관, 독일
베를린 | 2021/2020/2016 슈묵,
국제수공예박람회, 독일 뮌헨 | 2015
볼만 컬렉션, MAK, 오스트리아
비엔나
소장·수상·주요활동
푸른문화재단, 서울 | 볼만 컬렉션,

오스트리아 | 2021 선정, 소더비 옥션, 미국 | 2012 선정, 베를린, 뉴욕 전시작가, 독일 | 2011 입선, BKV-Prize, 독일 | 2007 입선, 탈렌테, 독일

현재
장신구 작가
samkac@me.com @sungcoco

Education
2014 Dpl. Meisterschülerin, Burg Giebichenstein Kunsthochschule Halle Germany | 2002 B.F.A. Ulsan university, Ulsan Korea
Solo Exhibitions
2019 Galeire Four, Goetheborg Schweden | 2018 Galeire Raon, Ulsan Korea | 2017 Galerie BIRO, Munich Germany
Group Exhibitions
2024 Remarks Beyound Ornament, SeMoCA, Seoul Korea | 2022 Ars Longa, Gallery SP, Seoul Korea | 2021 TWOxTWO for AIDS and Art, Dallas Museum of Art, Dallas USA | 2021 Frauen März, Tempelhof Schönberg Museum, Berlin Germany | 2021/2020/2016 SCHMUCK, IHM, Munich Germnay | 2015 Bollmann Collection, MAK, Wien Austria
Collections · Awards · Activities
Pureun Cultural Foundation, Korea | Bollmann Collection, Austria | 2021 Selected, Sothebye Auctions, USA | 2012 Selected, Berlin&NY Exchange artist, Germany | 2011 Selected, BKV-Prize, Germany | 2007 Selected, TALENTE, Germany
Present
Jewelry Artist
samkac@me.com, @sungcoco

송유경 Yookyung Song (1987–)
→58

학력
2023 서울대학교 박사 졸업, 서울 | 2016 에딘버러 대학교 대학원 졸업, 영국 | 2011 서울과학기술대학교 졸업, 서울
개인전
2023 수면, KCDF 윈도우 갤러리, 서울 | 2022 물결 속의 조각들, 갤러리 마룽, 서울 | 2021 혼재된 상, 갤러리 담, 서울
단체전
2024 LOOT MAD, 아트디자인박물관, 미국 뉴욕 | 2024 Empathy, The Gallery of

Art in Legnica, 폴란드 레그니차 | 2024 Gorgeous Jewellery 1.0, 디자인 상하이, 중국 상하이 | 2023 이타미 국제공예공모전, 이타미시립공예박물관, 일본 이타미
소장 · 수상 · 주요활동
2024 우승, LOOT MAD, 미국 | 2023 입선, 이타미 국제공예공모전, 일본 | 2023 입선, 레그니차 국제주얼리공모전, 폴란드 | 2023 선정, KCDF 공예 · 디자인 공모 신진작가부문, 서울
현재
장신구 작가
songyookyung@gmail.com, @songyookyung_jewellery

Education
2023 D.F.A. Seoul National University, Seoul Korea | 2016 M.F.A. Edinburgh College of Art, UK | 2011 B.F.A. Seoul National University of Science and Technology, Seoul Korea
Solo Exhibitions
2023 The Surface, KCDF Window Gallery, Seoul Korea | 2022 The Fragments in Water, Gallery Marron, Seoul Korea | 2021 Merged Images, Gallery Dam, Seoul Korea
Group Exhibitions
2024 LOOT MAD, Museum of Art and Design, NYC USA | 2024 Empathy, The Gallery of Art in Legnica, Legnica Poland | 2024 Gorgeous Jewellery 1.0, Design Shanghai, Shanghai China | 2023 ITAMI Int. Jewellery Exhibition, The Museum of Arts&Craft Itami, Itami Japan
Collections · Awards · Activities
2024 Winner, LOOT MAD, USA | 2023 Selected, ITAMI Int. Craft Competition, Japan | 2023 Selected, Legnica Int. Jewelry Competition, Poland | 2023 Selected, KCDF Young Artist in Craft and Design, Korea
Present
Jewelry Artist
songyookyung@gmail.com, @songyookyung_jewellery

심진아 Jina Sim (1980–)
→53

학력
2006 국민대학교 대학원 졸업, 서울 | 2003 동덕여자대학교 졸업, 서울
개인전
2013 낯설게 하기, KCDF 갤러리, 서울

단체전
2023 공예트렌드페어, 코엑스, 서울 | 2023 가로지르다, 갤러리 마쩨, 네덜란드 네이메헌 | 2018 키네시스-몸과 장식, 공근혜 갤러리, 서울 | 2016 페로몬-에로스의 과녁, 갤러리 다온, 서울 | 2014 컬렉트, 사치 갤러리, 영국 런던 | 2013 욕망하는 꽃, 갤러리 아트링크, 서울
소장 · 수상 · 주요활동
2008 입선, 포스코 스틸아트 어워드, 서울 | 2006 입선, 탈렌테, 독일
현재
장신구 작가
shimjinah@naver.com, @sim.sim.sim

Education
2006 M.F.A. Kookmin University, Seoul Korea | 2003 B.F.A. Dongduk Women's University, Seoul Korea
Solo Exhibitions
2013 Defamiliarization, KCDF Gallery, Seoul Korea
Group Exhibitions
2023 Craft Trend Fair, COEX, Seoul Korea | 2023 TRAVERSE, Galerie Marzee, Nijmegen Netherlands | 2018 Kinesis-Body and Ornament, Gallery Kong, Seoul Korea | 2016 Pheromone-Target Of Eros, Gallery Daon, Seoul Korea | 2014 COLLECT, Saatchi Gallery, London, UK | 2013 Flower of Desire, Gallery Artlink, Seoul Korea
Collections · Awards · Activities
2008 Selected, Posco Steel Art Award, Korea | 2006 Selected, TALENTE, Germany
Present
Jewelry Artist
shimjinah@naver.com, @sim.sim.sim

양지원 Jiwon Yang (1990–)
→123

학력
2018 국민대학교 대학원 졸업, 서울 | 2015 국민대학교 졸업, 서울
개인전
2022 소우주 마이너스, 아트포랩, 안양
단체전
2024 Inspired, 갤러리 엘, 서울 | 2024 BKV-Prize, 바이에른 미술공예협회, 독일 뮌헨 | 2023 표면의 정서, 갤러리 바움, 파주 | 2022 탈렌테, 국제수공예박람회, 독일 뮌헨 | 2018 마쩨 국제졸업작품전, 갤러리

마쩨, 네덜란드 네이메헌 | 2018 TRIPLE PARADE 비엔날레, 하우아트미술관, 중국 상하이
소장 · 수상 · 주요활동
2024 입선, BKV-Prize, 독일 | 2022 입선, 탈렌테, 독일 | 2022/2021 선정, 서울디자인페스티벌 영 디자이너, 서울 | 2018 입선, TRIPLE PARADE 비엔날레, 중국 | 2015 입선, BKV-Prize, 독일 | 2014 3등상, Ubi Top Young, 중국
현재
장신구 작가, 주얼리 브랜드 웨어드로잉 대표
weardrawing@naver.com, @yangjiyangji

Education
2018 M.F.A. Kookmin University, Seoul Korea | 2015 B.F.A. Kookmin University, Seoul Korea
Solo Exhibitions
2022 Microcosmos Minus, Art For Lab, Anyang Korea
Group Exhibitions
2024 Inspired, Gallery El, Seoul Korea | 2023 Texture External Sentiment, Gallery Baum, Paju Korea | 2022 TALENTE, IHM, Munich Germany | 2018 Marzee Int. Graduation Show, Galerie Marzee, Nijmegen Netherlands | 2018 4th Triple Parade Biennial, How Art Museum, Sanghai China
Collections · Awards · Activities
2024 Selected, BKV-Prize, Germany | 2022 Selected, TALENTE, Germany | 2022/2021 Selected, Seoul Design Festival Young Designer, Korea | 2018 Selected, TRIPLE PARADE Biennial, China | 2015 Selected, BKV-Prize, Germany | 2014 3rd Prize, Ubi Top Young, China
Present
Jewelry Artist, Director of Jewelry Brand Wear drawing
weardrawing@naver.com, @yangjiyangji

엄민재 Min-jae Eom (1993–)
→130

학력
2022 단국대학교 박사 수료, 천안 | 2020 뉴욕주립대학교 뉴팔츠 대학원 졸업, 미국 뉴욕 | 2018 단국대학교 졸업, 천안
개인전
2024 Archiving-memo, 갤러리 이즈, 서울 | 2021 Contact, KCDF 갤러리, 서울

단체전
2020 마쩨 국제졸업작품전, 갤러리 마쩨, 네덜란드 네이메헌 | 2020 Broken Beauty, 뮌헨 주얼리위크, 독일 뮌헨 | 2019 Broken Beauty, 알리아주 갤러리, 프랑스 릴 | 2019 Denizen 뉴욕시티주얼리위크, 프로스펙 하이츠, 미국 뉴욕 | 2019 Now Press Play, 미국 뉴욕 | 2018 Denizen 뉴욕시티주얼리위크, 첼시 호텔, 미국 뉴욕

현재
장신구 작가, 단국대학교 예술대학 미술학부 공예전공 초빙교수
jaeometal@dankook.ac.kr, www.minjaeeommetal.com, @g08jae

Education
2022 Ph.D. Candidate, Dankook University, Cheonan Korea | 2020 M.F.A. SUNY New Paltz, NY USA | 2018 B.F.A. Dankook University, Cheonan Korea
Solo Exhibitions
2024 Archiving-Memo, Gallery IS, Seoul Korea | 2021 Contact, KCDF Gallery, Seoul korea
Group Exhibitions
2020 Marzee Int. Graduate Show, Galerie Marzee, Nijmegen Netherlands | 2020 Broken Beauty, Munich Jewelry Week, Munich Germany | 2019 Broken Beauty, Alliages Gallery, Lille France | 2019 Denizen NYC Jewelry Week, Prospect Heights, NYC USA | 2019 Now Press Play, NY USA | 2018 Denizen NYC Jewelry Week, Chelsea Hotel, NYC USA
Present
Jewelry Artist, Visiting Professor, Dankook University, Cheonan Korea
djaalswo93@gmail.com, www.minjaeeommetal.com, @g08jae

엄세희 Sehee Um (1988–)   →33

학력
2017 서울대학교 대학원 졸업, 서울 | 2010 서울대학교 졸업, 서울
단체전
2024 DESIGNING IN JEWELLERY, 엘에비뉴 상하이 JCC 센터, 중국 상하이 | 2023 Harvest Perfume Soap Exhibition, 탬버린즈, 서울 | 2022 일품단장, 서울공예박물관 크래프트 윈도우, 서울 | 2021 수집으로부터,

Wang&Buck 갤러리, 덴마크 코펜하겐 | 2017 필라델피아미술관 공예전, 펜실베니아 컨벤션 센터, 미국 필라델피아
소장·수상·주요활동
2019 입선, 이타미 국제공예공모전, 일본 | 2018 탈렌테 상, 탈렌테, 독일
현재
장신구 작가
seheeum@gmail.com, @umsehee

Education
2017 M.F.A. Seoul National University, Seoul Korea | 2010 B.F.A. Seoul National University, Seoul Korea
Group Exhibitions
2024 DESIGNING IN JEWELLERY, L'Avenue Shanghai JCC Center, Shanghai China | 2023 Harvest Perfume Soap Exhibition, Tamburins, Seoul Korea | 2022 一品丹粧, SeMoCA, Seoul Korea | 2021 From Collect, Wang&Buck Gallery, Copenhagen Denmark | 2017 Philadelphia Museum of Art Craft Show, Pennsylvania Convention Center, Philadelphia USA
Collections·Awards·Activities
2019 Selected, ITAMI Int. Craft Competition, Japan | 2018 Talente Prize, TALENTE, Germany
Present
Jewelry Artist
seheeum@gmail.com, @umsehee

엄유진 Youjin Um (1976–)   →136

학력
2017 홍익대학교 대학원 졸업, 서울 | 2001 경기대학교 졸업, 수원
개인전
2024 만화경 속으로, 베나키 박물관샵, 그리스 아테네 | 2021 그림자 그 길, 킵인터치, 서울 | 2018 만화경, 갤러리 아원, 서울
단체전
2024 장식 너머 발언, 서울공예박물관, 서울 | 2024 허용할 수 없는 비밀, Werkstatt 갤러리, 독일 뮌헨 | 2024 AMBERIF, The Gallery of Art in Legnica, 앰버엑스포, 폴란드 그단스크 | 2024 Inhorgenta Munich QUALITY, 독일 뮌헨 | 2023 홍익금속조형회 해빙, 홍익대학교 현대미술관, 서울

소장·수상·주요활동
푸른문화재단, 서울 | 레그니차 미술관, 폴란드 | 2024 해외 부문 상, 제33회 일본 장신구공모전, 일본 | 2024 입선, 앰버 트립 아트장신구공모전 인클루시브, 리투아니아 | 2023 대상, 퀄리티 레그니차 국제주얼리공모전, 폴란드 | 2020 머티리얼 퀘스트 어워드, 아테네주얼리위크, 그리스
현재
장신구 및 오브제 작가
genei2001@gmail.com, @youjin_um

Education
2017 M.F.A. Hongik University, Seoul Korea | 2001 B.F.A. Kyonggi University, Suwon Korea
Solo Exhibitions
2024 Into the Kaleidoscope, Benaki Museum Shop, Athens Greece | 2021 Silhouette Road, Kit Craft Space, Seoul Korea | 2018 Kaleidoscope, Gallery Ahwon, Seoul Korea
Group Exhibitions
2024 Beyond Adornment, SeMoCA, Seoul Korea | 2024 (UN)Avowable Secrets, Werkstatt Gallery, Munich Germany | 2024 AMBERIF, The Gallery of Art in Legnica, AMBEREXPO, Gda sk Poland | 2024 Inhorgenta Munich QUALITY, Munich Germany | 2023 Hongik Metal Arts Association Thawing, Hongik University Museum of Modern Art, Seoul Korea
Collections·Awards·Activities
Pureun Cultural Foundation, Korea | The Gallery of Art in Legnica, Poland | 2024 Overseas Division Prize, 33th Japan Jewellery Competition, Japan | 2024 Selected, Amber Trip Art Jewellery Competition INCLUSIVE, Lithuania | 2023 Grand Prix, QUALITY Legnica Int. Jewellery Competition, Poland | 2020 Material Quest Award, Athens Jewelry Week, Greece
Present
Jewelry and Object Artist
genei2001@gmail.com, @youjin_um

원재선 Jaesun Won (1980–)   →116

학력
2022 서울과학기술대학교 박사 졸업, 서울 | 2008 로체스터

공과대학 대학원 졸업, 미국 로체스터
개인전
2020 정제된 차이 II, 갤러리 세인, 서울 | 2020 정제된 차이, 서울과학기술대학교 미술관, 서울 | 2017 Drawing Lines, KCDF 갤러리, 서울 외 2회
단체전
2023 만년사물, 서울공예박물관, 서울 | 2023 Contemporania, 팔라우 데 페드랄베스, 스페인 바르셀로나 | 2023 컬렉트, 영국 런던 | 2022 국제수공예박람회, 독일 뮌헨 | 2021 연리지 둘이서 하나이 되어, 아름지기, 서울 | 2019 LOOT MAD, 아트앤디자인박물관, 미국 뉴욕
소장·수상·주요활동
푸른문화재단, 서울 | 2023 올해의 금속공예가상, 서울 | 2021 특선, 청주국제공예공모전, 청주 | 2016 우승, NICHE 어워드 파인주얼리부분, 미국 | 2006 우승, 티파니 재단 어워드, 미국
현재
장신구 작가
jswjewelry@naver.com, @jaesun_won

Education
2022 Ph.D. Seoul National University of Science and Technology, Seoul Korea | 2008 M.F.A. Rochester Institute of Technology, USA
Solo Exhibitions
2020 Refined Difference II, GallerySein, Seoul Korea | 2020 Refined Difference, Seoul Tech Museum, Seoul Korea | 2017 Drawing Lines, Korean Craft&Design Foundation Gallery, Seoul Korea and 2 times
Group Exhibitions
2023 Long Lasting Objects of Metalsmiths, SeMoCA, Seoul Korea | 2023 Contemporania, Palau de Pedralbes, Barcelona Spain | 2023 COLLECT, London UK | 2022 IHM, Munich Germany | 2021 Yeonliji Two Becoming One, Arumjigi, Seoul Korea | 2019 LOOT MAD, Museum of Arts and Design, NYC USA
Collections·Awards·Activities
Pureun Cultural Foundation, Korea | 2023 Winner, Metalwork and Jewelry Award, Korea | 2021 Special Prize, Cheongju Int. Craft Competition, Korea |

2016 Winner, NICHE Award Fine Jewelry, USA | 2006 Winner, Tiffany Foundation Award, USA
Present
Jewelry Artist
jswjewelry@naver.com,
@jaesun_won

유다흰 Dahin Yoo (1994–) →142

학력
2023 성신여자대학교 대학원 졸업, 서울 | 2017 성신여자대학교 졸업, 서울
개인전
2023 공예트렌드페어-76년 후에 또 만나요, 코엑스, 서울 | 2023 to INFINITY, and BEYOND, KCDF 갤러리, 서울 | 2021 별들의 후손, KCDF 갤러리, 서울
단체전
2023 Opulent Handmade Treasures, Let's Curate, 미국 뉴욕 | 2023 모두의 미술, 모두의 컬렉션, 성신미술관, 서울 | 2022 THE MAXIMALIST.002, 크래프트온더힐, 서울 | 2021 그 겨울의 색, 스페이스 금채, 서울
소장·수상·주요활동
푸른문화재단, 서울
현재
공예가
hin0627@naver.com,
@dahinamic_

Education
2023 M.F.A. Sungshin University, Seoul Korea | 2017 B.F.A. Sungshin Women's University, Seoul Korea
Solo Exhibitions
2023 Crafts Trend Fair-See You Again in 76 Years, COEX, Seoul Korea | 2023 to INFINITY, and BEYOND, KCDF Gallery, Seoul Korea | 2021 Descendants of Stars, KCDF Gallery, Seoul Korea
Group Exhibitions
2023 Opulent Handmade Treasures, Let's Curate, NY USA | 2023 Everyone's Art, Everyone's Collection, Sungshin Museum of Art, Seoul Korea 2022 THE MAXIMALIST.002, Crafts on the hill, Seoul Korea | 2021 Color of the Winter, Space Keumchae, Seoul Korea
Collections·Awards·Activities
Pureun Cultural Foundation, Korea

Present
Craft Artist
hin0627@naver.com,
@dahinamic_

유아미 Ahmi Yu (1987–) →31

학력
2020 국민대학교 대학원 졸업, 서울 | 2016 국민대학교 졸업, 서울
단체전
2023 Of the garden's Earth&Air, 윤지박 갤러리, 미국 투손 | 2023 표면의 정서, 갤러리 바움, 파주 | 2022 마쩨 국제졸업작품전, 갤러리 마쩨, 네덜란드 네이메헌 | 2021 연리지 둘이서 하나이 되어, 아름지기, 서울 | 2020 사월의 장식, 통인화랑, 서울
소장·수상·주요활동
2022 마쩨 졸업작품상, 갤러리 마쩨, 네덜란드 | 2015 입선, 이타미 국제공예공모전, 일본
현재
장신구 작가
amyu354@gmail.com,
@_ami_yu

Education
2020 M.F.A. Kookmin University, Seoul | 2016 B.F.A. Kookmin University, Seoul
Group Exhibitions
2023 Of the garden's Earth&Air, Yun Gee Park Gallery, Tucson USA | 2023 Texture External Sentiment, Gallery Baum, Paju Korea | 2022 Marzee Int. Graduate Show, Galerie Marzee, Nijmegen Netherlands | 2021 Yeonliji Two Becoming one, Arumjigi, Seoul Korea | 2020 April Ornament, Tong In Gallery, Seoul Korea
Collections·Awards·Activities
2022 Marzee Graduate Prize, Galerie Marzee, Netherlands | 2015 Selected, ITAMI Int. Craft Competition, Japan
Present
Jewelry Artist
amyu354@gmail.com,
@_ami_yu

윤지예 Jiye Yun (1988–) →62

학력
2022 뮌헨 조형예술대학 졸업, 독일 뮌헨 | 2014 국민대학교 대학원 졸업, 서울 | 2012 국민대학교 졸업, 서울
단체전
2024 장식 너머 발언, 서울공예박물관, 서울 | 2024

Wellen Wogen Wirbel, 갤러리 한트베르크, 독일 뮌헨 | 2023 슈묵, 국제수공예박람회, 독일 뮌헨 | 2022 An Easterly Breeze, 갤러리 롭 카우데이스, 네덜란드 할렘 | 2022 Ars Longa, 갤러리 SP, 서울 | 2022 Tom&Jewellery, 쿤스트아카덴, 독일 뮌헨
소장·수상·주요활동
2023 1등상, BKV-Prize, 독일 | 2022 입선, Oberbayerischer Förderpreis für Angewandte Künste, 독일 | 2017 3등상, BKV-Prize, 독일 | 2015 입선, 탈렌테, 독일 | 2015 입선, 청주국제공예공모전, 청주
현재
장신구 작가
jiyeyun1029@gmail.com,
@jiyevvorks

Education
2022 Dpl. Akademie der Bildenden Künste, Munich Germany | 2014 M.F.A. Kookmin University, Seoul Korea | 2012 B.F.A. Kookmin University, Seoul Korea
Group Exhibitions
2024 Beyond Adornment, SeMoCA, Seoul Korea | 2024 Wellen WogenWirbel, Galerie Handwerk, Munich Germany | 2023 SCHMUCK, IHM, Munich Germany | 2022 An Easterly Breeze, Gallery Rob Koudijs, Haarlem Netherlands | 2022 Ars Longa, Gallery SP, Seoul Korea | 2022 Tom&Jewellery, Kunstarkaden, Munich Germany
Collections·Awards·Activities
2023 1st Prize, BKV-Prize, Germany | 2022 Selected, Oberbayerischer Förderpreis für Angewandte Künste, Germany | 2017 3rd Prize, BKV-Prize, Germany | 2015 Selected, TALENTE, Germany | 2015 Selected, Cheongju Int. Craft Competition, Korea
Present
Jewelry Artist
jiyeyun1029@gmail.com,
@jiyevvorks

이나진 Najin Lee (1989–) →132

학력
2021 성신여자대학교 대학원 졸업, 서울 | 2015 성신여자대학교 졸업, 서울

개인전
2018 바람이 노래를 불러주었다, 갤러리 아원, 서울
단체전
2023 정원산책, 갤러리 완물, 서울 | 2021 블루 불확실한 봄, 갤러리 바움, 파주 | 2020 몸에 그리는 그림, 갤러리 바움, 파주 | 2019 뜰에 깃들, 이유진 갤러리, 서울 | 2019 JOYA 현대장신구박람회, 디자인허브, 스페인 바르셀로나 | 2018 TRIPLE PARADE, 하우아트미술관, 중국 상하이
소장·수상·주요활동
바르셀로나 디자인박물관, 스페인 | 2019 입선, 슈묵, 독일 | 2018 우승, ENJOIA'T, 스페인 | 2018 입선, 탈렌테, 독일
현재
장신구 및 금속공예 작가
nanazin@naver.com,
@nananazin

Education
2021 M.F.A. SungShin University, Seoul Korea | 2015 B.F.A. SungShin Women's University, Seoul Korea
Solo Exhibitions
2018 The wind gave a song, Gallery Ahwon, Seoul Korea
Group Exhibitions
2023 Walk in the garden, Gallery Wanmul, Seoul Korea | 2021 Blue An Uncertain Spring, Gallery Baum, Paju Korea | 2020 Drawing on the body, Gallery Baum, Paju Korea | 2019 Nest in a Garden, Lee Eugean Gallery, Seoul | 2019 JOYA Art Jewellery&Objects Fair, Disseny Hub,, Barcelona Spain | 2018 TRIPLE PARADE, HOW art Museum, Shanghai China
Collections·Awards·Activities
Design Museum of Barcelona, Spain | 2019 Selected, SCHMUCK, Germany | 2018 Winner, ENJOIA'T, Spain | 2018 Selected, TALENTE, Germany
Present
Jewelry and Metalwork Artist
nanazin@naver.com,
@nananazin

이남경 Namkyung Lee (1985–) →98

학력
2016 국민대학교 디자인대학원 졸업, 서울

개인전
2022 이미지 룸, 무목적, 서울 |
2022 이남경 개인전, 갤러리 Alice
Floriano, 브라질 포르투알레그리
| 2022 이미지 아카이브, KCDF
윈도우 갤러리, 서울 | 2021 이미지
아카이브, 갤러리 아원, 서울
단체전
2024 장식 너머 발언,
서울공예박물관, 서울 | 2023
Just Art! Beyond Borders,
플랫폼엘, 서울 | 2021 JOYA
아트주얼리&오브젝트,
디자인박물관, 스페인
바르셀로나 | 2019 LOOT MAD,
아트앤디자인박물관, 미국 뉴욕
소장·수상·주요활동
2021 우승, Arte y Joya, 스페인
| 2021 특선, Enjoia't, 스페인
| 2020 JOYA 어워드, JOYA
아트주얼리&오브젝트, 스페인
| 2020 가작, 뉴 타이페이 시티
국제금속공예공모전, 대만 | 2020
입선, Gioielli in Fermento,
이탈리아
현재
장신구 작가
nkjewelrystudio@gmail.com,
www.nkjewellerystudio.com,
@namkyung_lee

Education
2016 M.F.A. Graduate School
of Design Kookmin University,
Seoul Korea
Solo Exhibitions
2022 IMAGE ROOM,
Mumokjeok, Seoul Korea | 2022
Namkyung Lee Solo Exhibition,
Galeria Alice Floriano,
PortoAlegre Brasil | 2022 Image
Archive, KCDF Window Gallery,
Seoul Korea | 2021 Image
Archive, Gallery Ahwon, Seoul
Korea
Group Exhibitions
2024 Beyond Adornment,
SeMoCA, Seoul Korea | 2023
Just Art! Beyond Borders,
Platform-L, Seoul Korea | 2021
JOYA Art Jewellery&Objects
Fair, Museu del Disseny,
Barcelona Spain | 2019 LOOT
MAD, Museum of Arts and
Design, NYC USA
Collections·Awards·Activities
2021 Winner, Arte y Joya,
Spain | 2021 First Finalist,
Enjoia't, Spain | 2020 JOYA
Award, JOYA Barcelona Art
Jewellery&Objects, Spain |
2020 Honorable Mention, New

Taipei City Int. Metal Crafts
Competition, Taiwan | 2020
Selected, Gioielli in Fermento,
Italy
Present
Jewelry Artist
nkjewelrystudio@gmail.com,
www.nkjewellerystudio.com,
@namkyung_lee

이선용 Seonyong Lee (1984–)
→128

학력
2022 서울대학교 박사 졸업, 서울 |
2013 사바나 미술대학 대학원 졸업,
미국 사바나 | 2006 홍익대학교
졸업, 서울
개인전
2020 Silly Silicone, 무목적, 서울
| 2020 Cast Skin Series, KCDF
윈도우 갤러리, 서울 | 2019 Cast
Skin Series, 갤러리 코소, 서울
단체전
2024 Gorgeous Jewellery 1.0,
디자인 상하이, 중국 상하이 | 2024
프레임, 국제수공예박람회, 독일 뮌헨
| 2024 Collect, 서머셋 하우스,
영국 런던 | 2023 오브제가 된 사물,
KCDF 갤러리, 서울 | 2022 Ars
Longa, 갤러리 SP, 서울 | 2022
공예 춘색, 서울공예박물관 크래프트
윈도우, 서울 | 2022 공예가의
자급자족, 다다손손, 서울
소장·수상·주요활동
푸른문화재단, 서울
현재
장신구 및 오브제 작가
seonyong112@gmail.com,
seonyongleejewelry.com,
@seonyongleejewelry

Education
2022 D.F.A. Seoul National
University, Seoul Korea | 2013
M.F.A. Savannah College of Art
and Design, Savannah USA |
2006 B.F.A. Hongik University,
Seoul Korea
Solo Exhibitions
2020 Silly Silicone, Mumokjeok,
Seoul Korea | 2020 Cast Skin
Series, KCDF Window Gallery,
Seoul Korea | 2019 Cast Skin
Series, Gallery COSO, Seoul
Korea
Group Exhibitions
2024 Gorgeous Jewellery 1.0,
Design Shanghai, Shanghai
China | 2024 FRAME, IHM,
Munich Germany | 2024 Collect,
Somerset House, London UK |

2023 Objets and Objects, KCDF
Gallery, Seoul Korea | 2022 Ars
Longa, Gallery SP, Seoul Korea
| 2022 Craft Colors of Spring,
SeMoCA Craft Window, Seoul
Korea | 2022 Self Sufficiency of
Craftsmen, Dadasonson, Seoul
Korea
Collections·Awards·Activities
Pureun Cultural Foundation,
Korea
Present
Jewelry and Object Artist
seonyong112@gmail.com,
seonyongleejewelry.com,
@seonyongleejewelry

이소리 Sohri Yi (1982–)
→94

학력
2008 경기대학교 졸업, 수원
단체전
2024 장식 너머 발언,
서울공예박물관, 서울 | 2024
프레임, 국제수공예박람회, 갤러리
오, 독일 뮌헨 | 2023 프레임,
국제수공예박람회, 갤러리 오,
독일 뮌헨 | 2021 공예트렌드페어-
주제관전시, 코엑스, 서울 | 2020
Absolutely Abstract, 이유진
갤러리, 서울 | 2020 HAN made,
CCBC 갤러리, 캐나다 벤쿠버
| 2019 SOFA, 노엘 기요마르크
갤러리, 미국 시카고
소장·수상·주요활동
댈러스미술관, 미국
현재
장신구 작가
sohriyi@gmail.com, @yi_sohri

Education
2008 B.F.A. Kyonggi University,
Suwon Korea
Group Exhibitions
2024 Beyond Adornment,
SeMoCA, Seoul Korea | 2024
FRAME, IHM, Gallery O, Munich
Germany | 2023 FRAME, IHM,
Gallery O, Munich Germany
| 2021 Craft Trend Fair Main
Exhibition, Coex, Seoul Korea |
2020 Absolutely Abstract, Lee
Eugean Gallery, Seoul Korea
| 2020 HAN made, CCBC
Gallery, Vancouver Canada
| 2019 SOFA Chicago, Gallery
Noel Guyomarc'h, Chicago
USA
Collections·Awards·Activities
Dallas Museum of Art, USA
Present
Jewelry Artist
sohriyi@gmail.com, @yi_sohri

이승열 Sungyeoul Lee (1977–)
→40

학력
2008 일리노이대학교 대학원 졸업,
미국 일리노이 | 2003 국민대학교
졸업, 서울
개인전
2018 나의 반쪽, 마크A. 채프만
갤러리, 미국 맨해튼 | 2015 같지만
다른, 갤러리 담, 서울 | 2013 내재된
가치, 안나 르노웬스 갤러리, 캐나다
할리팩스 | 2011 친밀함, 마크A.
채프만 갤러리, 미국 맨해튼
단체전
2024 장식 너머 발언,
서울공예박물관, 서울 | 2023
장식적 디지털리즘 II, 템플
컨템포러리, 미국 필라델피아 |
2023 청주공예비엔날레-사물의
지도, 청주문화제조장, 청주 | 2023
별주구전, 갤러리 완물, 서울 | 2023
가로지르다, 갤러리 마쩨, 네덜란드
네이메헌
소장·수상·주요활동
고척 아이파크, 한국 | 운정 아이파크,
한국 | 스파르타 티팟 뮤지엄,
미국 | 청주 국제공예비엔날레
조직위원회, 한국 | 2016/2012 은상,
사울벨디자인어워드, 미국 | 2023
전시기획, 장식적 디지털리즘 II, 미국
현재
금속공예가, 국민대학교 조형대학
금속공예학과 조교수
seunglee@kookmin.ac.kr,
@sungyeoul_lee

Education
2008 M.F.A. University of
Illinois, Illinois USA | 2003 B.F.A.
Kookmin University, Seoul
Korea
Solo Exhibitions
2018 My Other Half, Mark A.
Chapman Gallery, Manhattan
USA | 2015 Same Same but
Different, Gallery Dam, Seoul
Korea | 2013 Body Ornament-
Implicit Value, Anna Leonowens
Gallery, Halifax Canada | 2011
Intimacy, Mark A. Chapman
Gallery, Manhattan USA
Group Exhibitions
2024 Beyond Adornment,
SeMoCA, Seoul Korea | 2023
Decorative Digitalism II, Temple
Contemporary, Philadelphia
USA | 2023 Cheongju Craft
Biennale, Culture Factory,
Cheongju Korea | 2023 Odd
Bottle, Gallery Wannmul, Seoul

Korea | 2023 TRAVERSE, Galerie Marzee, Nijmegen Netherlands
Collections·Awards·Activities
Gocheok I-Park, Korea | Unjeong I-Park, Korea | Sparta Teapot Museum, USA | Cheongju Craft Biennale Organizing Committee, Korea | 2016/2012 Silver Prize, Saul bell Design Award, USA | 2023 Curated, Decorative Digitalism II, USA
Present
Metalsmith, Assistant Professor, Kookmin University, Seoul Korea
seunglee@kookmin.ac.kr, @sungyeoul_lee

이영주 Youngjoo Lee (1975–) →22

학력
2010 서울대학교 대학원 졸업, 서울 | 2000 건국대학교 졸업, 서울
개인전
2021 카논 호흡의 음률, KCDF 갤러리, 서울 | 2019 카논 규칙과 변주, 갤러리 아원, 서울 외 3회
단체전
2023 만년사물, 서울공예박물관, 서울 | 2023 다시, 자연에게 보내는 편지, 문화역서울284, 서울 | 2022 롯데아트페어, 시그니엘부산, 부산 | 2021 Artistry Re-imagined, Spotlight on the East, CKA, 미국 뉴욕 | 2019 국제수공예박람회, 독일 뮌헨
소장·수상·주요활동
서울공예박물관, 서울 | 푸른문화재단, 서울 | 2020 올해의 금속공예가상, 서울 | 2010 선정, NTJ 어워즈, 네덜란드 | 2009 은상, 삼신국제다이아몬드 주얼리디자인공모전, 서울 | 2019 전시기획, 애착의 물건, 서울
현재
장신구 작가, 금속공예가
lyj582020@naver.com, @youngjooleee

Education
2010 M.F.A. Seoul National University, Seoul Korea | 2000 B.F.A. Konkuk University, Seoul Korea
Solo Exhibitions
2021 Kanon Rhythm of breathing, KCDF Gallery, Seoul Korea | 2019 Kanon Rules and Variations, Gallery Ahwon, Seoul Korea and 3 times

Group Exhibitions
2023 Long Lasting Objects of Metalsmiths, SeMoCA, Seoul Korea | 2023 Again, A Letter To Nature, Culture Station Seoul 284, Seoul Korea | 2022 Lotte Art Fair Busan, Signiel Busan, Busan Korea | 2021 Artistry Re-imagined, Spotlight on the East, CKA, NYC USA | 2019 IHM, Munich Germany
Collections·Awards·Activities
SeMoCA, Korea | Pureun Cultural Foundation, Korea | 2020 Winner, Metalwork and Jewelry Award, Korea | 2010 Selected, NTJ Awards, Netherlands | 2008 Silver Prize, Samshin Int. Jewelry Design Awards, Korea | 2019 Curated, RE:love objects, Korea
Present
Jewelry Artist, Metalsmith
lyj582020@naver.com, @youngjooleee

이재현 Jaehyun Lee (1988–) →90

학력
2019 국민대학교 대학원 졸업, 서울 | 2015 인하대학교 졸업, 인천
단체전
2023 Midnight! Crown Shyness, 갤러리 아원, 서울 | 2021 Crown shyness, 갤러리 아원, 서울 | 2021 블루 불확실한 봄, 갤러리 바움, 파주 | 2020 몸에 그리는 그림, 갤러리 바움, 파주 | 2019 마쩨 국제졸업작품전, 갤러리 마쩨, 네덜란드 네이메헌
현재
장신구 작가
01117189222@naver.com, @whistle_moon

Education
2019 M.F.A. Kookmin University, Seoul Korea | 2015 B.F.A. Inha University, Incheon Korea
Group Exhibitions
2023 Midnight! Crown Shyness, Gallery Ahwon, Seoul Korea | 2021 Crown shyness, Gallery Ahwon, Seoul Korea | 2021 Blue An Uncertain Spring, Gallery Baum, Paju Korea | 2020 Drawing on the body, Gallery Baum, Paju Korea | 2019 Marzee Int. Graduate Show, Galerie Marzee, Nijmegen Netherlands
Present
Jewelry Artist
01117189222@naver.com, @whistle_moon

이주현 Joohyun Lee (1974–) →60

학력
2005 건국대학교 대학원 졸업, 서울 | 1997 건국대학교 졸업, 충주
개인전
2019 접점, 산울림 아트앤크래프트, 서울 | 2013 미소 갤러리, 서울 | 2010 갤러리 이듬, 부산 | 2009 Circlet, 갤러리 아신, 서울 | 2008 빨강, 갤러리카페 빨강숲, 서울 | 2007 여행 떠나고 머물다, 스페이스 두루, 서울
단체전
2020 LA Art Show, 로스앤젤레스 컨벤션센터, 미국 로스앤젤레스 | 2020 Absolutely Abstract, 이유진 갤러리, 서울 | 2019 SOFA 시카고, 샤론 크란센 아트, 미국 시카고 | 2019 JOYA 아트주얼리&오브젝트, 디자인박물관, 스페인 바르셀로나
소장·수상·주요활동
2024 현대공예 소장자료 연구 및 해제, 서울공예박물관, 서울 | 2017 예술강사 금속프로그램 교육연구, 한국문화예술교육진흥원, 서울 | 2013 공예 디자인 인력양성 기반구축 연구, KCDF, 서울
현재
장신구 스튜디오 hyun炫 운영 건국대학교 예술디자인대학 리빙디자인학과 겸임교수, 서울
jhmind@hanmail.net, @jhlee0919

Education
2005 M.F.A. Konkuk University, Seoul Korea | 1997 B.F.A. Konkuk University, Chungju Korea
Solo Exhibitions
2019 The Point of Contact, Sanwoollim Art&Craft, Seoul Korea | 2013 Miso Gallery, Seoul Korea | 2010 Gallery Idm, Busan Korea | 2009 Circlet, Gallery A-Shin, Seoul Korea | 2008 The Red, Gallery cafe Palgangsup, Seoul Korea | 2007 Travel Leave and Stay, Gallary Duru, Seoul Korea
Group Exhibitions
2020 LA Art Show, Los Angeles Convention Center, LA USA | 2020 Absolutely Abstract, Lee Eugean Gallery, Seoul Korea | 2019 SOFA Chicago, Charon Kranson Art, Chicago USA | 2019 JOYA Art Jewellery&Objects Fair, Museu del Disseny, Barcelona Spain

Collections·Awards·Activities
2024 Research on the Collections of Contemporary Crafts, SeMoCA, Korea | 2017 Program Research and Education for Art Instructor, Korea Art&Culture Education Service, Korea | 2013 Research of Human Resource Development Foundation Construction on Crafts Design, KCDF, Korea
Present
Director of hyun炫 Jewelry Studio, Adjunct Professor, Department of Living Design, Konkuk University, Seoul Korea
jhmind@hanmail.net, @jhlee0919

이진경 Jinkyung Lee (1979–)
→105

학력
2019 한양대학교 박사수료, 서울 | 2011 제네바예술대학교 졸업, 스위스 제네바 | 2007 한양대학교 대학원 졸업, 서울 | 2004 한양대학교 졸업, 안산
개인전
2013 Dentelle revistée, 갤러리 담, 서울
단체전
2021 ㅅ·ㅎ·ㄱ-色形感 장신구전, 스페이스 금채, 서울 | 2017 오너먼테이션, 유리지공예관, 서울 | 2013 장식과 환영, 국립현대미술관, 과천
소장·수상·주요활동
푸른문화재단, 서울
현재
장신구 작가, 한양대학교 디자인대학 주얼리패션디자인학과 겸임교수, 안산
jlee.bijou@gmail.com, @jinkyunglee_

Education
2019 Ph.D. Candidate, Hanyang University, Seoul Korea | 2011 Dpl. Geneva University of Art and Design, Jeneva Switzerland | 2007 M.F.A. Hanyang University, Seoul Korea | 2004 B.F.A. Hanyang University, Ansan Korea
Solo Exhibitions
2013 Dentelle revistée, Gallery Dam, Seoul Korea
Group Exhibitions
2021 C·F·S, Space Keumchae, Seoul Korea
2017 Ornamentation, Yoolizzy

Craft Museum, Seoul Korea | 2013 Ornament and Illusion, MMCA, Gwacheon Korea
Collections·Awards·Activities
Pureun Cultural Foundation, Korea
Present
Jewelry Artist, Affiliated Professor, Hanyang University, Ansan Korea
jlee.bijou@gmail.com,
@jinkyunglee_

이형찬 Hyungchan Lee (1997-)
→110

학력
2023 국민대학교 대학원 졸업, 서울 | 2020 건국대학교 졸업, 충주
개인전
2023 공예트렌드페어, 코엑스, 서울
단체전
2024 ESCAPERS AN OTHER WORLDS, 갤러리 이스케이퍼, 일본 도쿄 | 2024 프레임, 국제수공예박람회, 갤러리 오, 독일 뮌헨 | 2024 (UN)Avowable Secrets, 알리아주 갤러리, 독일 뮌헨 | 2023 이타미 국제공예전, 이타미 시립공예박물관, 일본 이타미
소장·수상·주요활동
2023 2등상, 이타미 국제공예공모전, 일본
현재
장신구 및 오브제 작가
ggudcks97@naver.com,
www.hyungchanlee.com,
@hyungchanleee

Education
2023 M.F.A. Kookmin University, Seoul Korea | 2020 B.F.A. Konkuk University, Chungju Korea
Solo Exhibitions
2023 Craft Trend Fair, COEX, Seoul Korea
Group Exhibitions
2024 ESCAPERS AN OTHER WORLDS, Gallery Escapers, Tokyo Japan | 2024 FRAME, IHM, Gallery O, Munich Germany | 2024 (UN)Avowable Secrets, Alliages Gallary, Munich Germany | 2023 ITAMI Int. Craft Exhibition, The Museum of Arts&Craft, Itami Japan
Collections·Awards·Activities
2023 2nd Best Overall Award, ITAMI Int. Craft Competition, Japan
Present
Jewelry and Object Artist

ggudcks97@naver.com,
www.hyungchanlee.com,
@hyungchanleee

임제운 Jewoon Lim (1995-)   →50

학력
2023 국민대학교 대학원 졸업, 서울 | 2019 중앙대학교 졸업, 서울
단체전
2024 집, 갤러리 아원, 서울 | 2024 탈렌테, 국제수공예박람회, 독일 뮌헨 | 2023 마쩨 국제졸업작품전, 갤러리 마쩨, 네덜란드 | 2023 감각의 기억, PRGM 스페이스, 서울 | 2023 Jewelry and Travel, 틴칼 랩, 포르투갈 포르투 | 2020 ON THE DESK, 갤러리 아원, 서울
소장·수상·주요활동
2024 입선, 탈렌테, 독일 | 2023 마쩨 졸업작품상, 갤러리 마쩨, 네덜란드
현재
장신구 작가, 닷츠 스튜디오 대표
dots_korea@naver.com,
@tary_ism

Education
2023 M.F.A. Kookmin University, Seoul Korea | 2019 B.F.A. Chungang University, Seoul Korea
Group Exhibitions
2024 Home, Gallery Ahwon, Seoul Korea | 2024 TALENTE, IHM, Munich Germany | 2023 Marzee Int. Graduate Show, Galerie Marzee, Nijmegen Netherlands | 2023 Experience, Remember, PRGM SPACE, Seoul Korea | 2023 Jewelry and Travel, Tincal Lab, Porto Portugal | 2020 ON THE DESK, Gallery Ahwon, Seoul Korea
Collections·Awards·Activities
2024 Selected, TALENTE, Germany | 2023 Marzee Graduate Prize, Galerie Marzee, Netherlands
Present
Jewelry Artist, Director of DOTS studio
dots_korea@naver.com,
@tary_ism

임종석 Jongseok Lim (1987-) →103

학력
2016 국민대학교 대학원 졸업, 서울 | 2013 건국대학교 졸업, 충주
개인전
2023 태고의 춤, 아트 스페이스W, 서울 | 2022 휴화의 바다, 플레이스

막1, 서울 외 3회
단체전
2024 장식 너머 발언, 서울공예박물관, 서울 | 2023 Of the Garden's Earth&Air, 윤지박 갤러리, 미국 투손 | 2023 Contemporania, 팔라우 데 페드랄베스, 스페인 바르셀로나 | 2021 연리지 둘이서 하나 되어, 아름지기, 서울
소장·수상·주요활동
서울공예박물관, 서울 | 푸른문화재단, 서울 | V&A 박물관, 영국 | CODA 박물관, 네덜란드 | 스헤르토헨보스 디자인박물관, 네덜란드 | 2019 우승, Preziosa Young 디자인공모전, 이탈리아 | 2016 공예트렌드페어 올해의 작가상, 서울
현재
장신구 작가
ka_fka@naver.com,
@jongseoklim_artjewelry

Education
2016 M.F.A. Kookmin University, Seoul Korea | 2013 B.F.A. Konkuk University, Chungju Korea
Solo Exhibitions
2023 Ancient Travels, Art Space W, Seoul Korea | 2022 The Dormant Sea, Place Mak1, Seoul Korea and 3 times
Group Exhibitions
2024 Beyond Adornment, SeMoCA, Seoul Korea | 2023 Of the Garden's Earth&Air, Yun Gee Park Gallery, Tucson USA | 2023 Contemporania, Palau de Pedralbes, Barcelona Spain | 2021 Yeonliji Two Becoming One, Arumjigi, Seoul Korea
Collections·Awards·Activities
SeMoCA, Korea | Pureun Cultural Foundation, Korea | V&A Museum, UK | CODA Museum, Netherlands | Design Museum Den Bosch, Netherlands | 2019 Winner, Preziosa Young Design Competition, Italy | 2016 Craft Trend Fair Artist of the Year, Korea
Present
Jewelry Artist
ka_fka@naver.com,
@jongseoklim_artjewelry

장지영 Jiyoung Jang (1988-)   →138

학력
2018 국민대학교 대학원 졸업, 서울 |

2012 국민대학교 졸업, 서울
단체전
2024 (UN)Avowable Secrets, 알리아주 갤러리, 독일 뮌헨 | 2023 표면의 정서, 갤러리 바움, 파주 | 2020 탈렌테, 국제수공예박람회, 독일 뮌헨 | 2019 오월의 시, 유리지공예관, 서울 | 2018 TRIPLE PARADE, 하우아트미술관, 중국 상하이
소장·수상·주요활동
2020 입선, 탈렌테, 독일 | 2015 입선, 이타미 국제공예공모전, 일본
현재
장신구 작가
semi0113@gmail.com,
@jiyoungj__

Education
2018 M.F.A. Kookmin University, Seoul Korea | 2012 B.F.A. Kookmin University, Seoul Korea
Group Exhibitions
2024 (UN)Avowable Secrets, Alliages Gallary, Munich Germany | 2023 Texture External Sentiment, Gallery Baum, Paju Korea | 2020 TALENTE, IHM, Munich Germany | 2019 Poems for May, Yoolizzy Craft Museum, Seoul Korea | 2018 TRIPLE PARADE, HOW Art Museum, Shanghai China
Collections·Awards·Activities
2020 Selected, TALENTE, Germany | 2015 Selected, ITAMI Int. Craft Competition, Japan
Present
Jewelry Artist
semi0113@gmail.com,
@jiyoungj__

조완희 Wanhee Cho (1983-)   →134

학력
2022 홍익대학교 박사 졸업, 서울 | 2016 샌디에이고 주립대학 대학원 졸업, 미국 샌디에이고 | 2012 로드아일랜드 스쿨오브디자인 대학원 수료, 미국 프로비던스 | 2010 로체스터 공과대학교 졸업, 미국 로체스터
개인전
2023 Illusion Fantasy, 미드나잇 아트 갤러리, 서울 | 2022 Unfamiliar Familiarity, 크래프트온더힐, 서울 | 2021 In·Visible, 공근혜 갤러리, 서울 | 2021 Le Pli, 스페이스 오매 갤러리,

---

서울 | 2018 Tender Tenacity, 갤러리 아원, 서울 | 2016 Sense of Wonder, 더 유니버시티 갤러리, 미국 샌디에이고
단체전
2023 장식적 디지털리즘 II, 템플 컨템포러리, 미국 필라델피아 | 2023 아트페스타인제주, 산지천 갤러리, 제주 | 2019 사랑방, 노엘 기요마르크 갤러리, 캐나다 몬트리올 | 2019 프레임, 국제수공예박람회, 독일 뮌헨
소장·수상·주요활동
Permanent Preziosa Young 콜렉션, 이탈리아 | San Diego State University 콜렉션, 미국 | 2013 우승, Preziosa Young 어워드, 이탈리아
현재
장신구 작가, 단국대학교 예술대학 미술학부 공예전공 조교수, 천안
wanycraft@gmail.com,
@wanycraft

Education
2022 Ph.D. Hongik University, Seoul Korea | 2016 M.F.A. San Diego State University, San Diego USA | 2012 M.F.A. Candidate, Rhode Island School of Design, Providence USA | 2010 B.F.A. Rochester Institute of Technology, Rochester USA
Solo Exhibitions
2023 Illusion Fantasy, Midnight Art Gallery, Seoul Korea | 2022 Unfamiliar Familiarity, Crafts On The Hill Gallery, Seoul Korea | 2021 In·Visible, Gallery KONG, Seoul Korea | 2021 Le Pli, Space OMAE Gallery, Seoul Korea | 2018 Tender Tenacity, Gallery Ahwon, Seoul Korea | 2016 Sense of Wonder, The University Gallery, San Diego USA
Group Exhibitions
2023 Decorative Digitalism II, Temple Contemporary, Philadelphia USA | 2023 Art Festa in Jeju, SJC Gallery, Jeju Korea | 2019 SARANGBANG, Galerie Noel Guyomarc'h, Montreal Canada | 2019 FRAME, IHM, Munich Germany
Collections·Awards·Activities
Permanent Preziosa Young Collection, Italy | San Diego State University Collection, USA | 2013 Winner, Preziosa Young Award, Italy
Present
Jewelry Artist, Assistant Professor, Dankook University, Cheonan Korea

wanycraft@gmail.com,
@wanycraft

진유리 Yuri Jin (1981–)   →112
학력
2012 홍익대학교 대학원 졸업, 서울 | 2005 홍익대학교 졸업, 서울
개인전
2014 Daily Life, KCDF 갤러리, 서울 | 2011 Cube, SASS 갤러리, 서울
단체전
2024 Wearing Red, 파티나 갤러리, 미국 샌타페이 | 2023 청주국제공예공모전, 문화제조창, 청주 | 2013 The land of the morning calm, 아틀리에, 프랑스 파리 | 2012 50 Brooch Ideas, 스페이스 두루, 서울 | 2011 공·공의 방, 서교예술실험센터, 서울
소장·수상·주요활동
2023 입선, 청주국제공예공모전, 청주 | 2015 금속공예 워크샵, 콩코디아 대학, 미국 | 2011 신당창작아케이드2기 입주작가
현재
장신구 작가
jinyuri3883@gmail.com,
@jinyuri_jewelry

Education
2012 M.F.A. Hongik University, Seoul Korea | 2005 B.F.A. Hongik University, Seoul Korea
Solo Exhibitions
2014 Daily Life, KCDF Gallery, Seoul Korea | 2011 Cube, SASS, Seoul Korea
Group Exhibitions
2024 Wearing Red, Patina Gallery, Santa Fe USA | 2023 Cheongju Int. Craft Competition, Culture Factory, Cheongju Korea | 2013 The land of the morning calm, L'Atelier, Paris France | 2012 50 Brooch Ideas, space duru, Seoul Korea | 2011 The room of Gong-gong, Seoul Art Space Seogyo, Seoul Korea
Collections·Awards·Activities
2023 Selected, Cheongju Int. Craft Competition, Korea | 2015 Concordia College, Metal Art Workshop, USA | 2011 SASS, Artist in Residence, Korea
Present
Jewelry Artist
jinyuri3883@gmail.com,
@jinyuri_jewelry

최예진 Ye-jin Choi (1996–)   →92
학력
2022 국민대학교 대학원 졸업, 서울 | 2019 국민대학교 졸업, 서울
개인전
2024 봄의 조각, KCDF 윈도우 갤러리, 서울 | 2023 공예트렌드페어, 코엑스, 서울 | 2022 공예트렌드페어, 코엑스, 서울 | 2022 In Full Bloom, 갤러리 아미디, 서울
단체전
2024 기호공감, 갤러리 인사아트, 서울 | 2024 크래프트 서울, 코엑스, 서울 | 2023 이타미 국제공예전, 이타미 시립공예박물관, 일본 이타미 | 2023 표면의 정서, 갤러리 바움, 파주 | 2022 ASIA MON AMOUR, NYC Fringe, 미국 뉴욕
소장·수상·주요활동
2023 입선, 이타미 국제공예공모전, 일본
현재
장신구 작가
yejinny9611@gmail.com,
@yejinny__work

Education
2022 M.F.A. Kookmin University, Seoul Korea | 2019 B.F.A. Kookmin University, Seoul Korea
Solo Exhibitions
2024 Piece of Spring, KCDF Window Gallery, Seoul Korea | 2023 Craft Trend Fair, COEX, Seoul Korea | 2022 Craft Trend Fair, COEX, Seoul Korea | 2022 In Full Bloom, Gallery Amidi, Seoul Korea
Group Exhibitions
2024 Empathy with Sense, Gallery Insaart, Seoul Korea | 2024 Craft Seoul, Coex, Seoul Korea | 2023 ITAMI Int. Craft Exhibition, The Museum of Arts&Crafts, Itami Japan | 2023 Texture External Sentiment, Gallery Baum, Paju Korea | 2022 ASIA MON AMOUR, NYC Fringe, NYC USA
Collections·Awards·Activities
2023 Selected, ITAMI Int. Craft Competition, Japan
Present
Jewelry Artist
yejinny9611@gmail.com,
@yejinny__work

최윤정 Yoonjung Choi (1982–)   →100
학력
2022 홍익대학교 박사 졸업, 서울 | 2010 홍익대학교 대학원 졸업, 서울 | 2001 홍익대학교 졸업, 서울
개인전
2021 The Breath Pouch, 크래프트온더힐, 서울 | 2020 숨, 그 부피의 조각, 갤러리 아원, 서울 | 2019 공예트렌드페어-숨, 그 부피의 조각, 코엑스, 서울 | 2013 Figure+structure, 57th 갤러리, 서울 외 3회
단체전
2023 장식적 디지털리즘 II, 템플 컨템포러리, 미국 필라델피아 | 2023 청주공예비엔날레-사물의 지도, 청주문화제조창, 청주 | 2022 Ars Longa, 갤러리 SP, 서울 | 2021 공예트렌드페어, 코엑스, 서울
소장·수상·주요활동
서울공예박물관, 서울 | 2020 입선, Arte y Joya 국제주얼리공모전, 스페인 | 2020 가작, 뉴 타이베이 시티 국제금속공예공모전, 대만 | 2019 심사위원상, 이타미 국제공예공모전, 일본
현재
장신구 작가, 한양대학교 주얼리·패션디자인과 겸임교수, 안산, 홍익대학교 금속조형디자인과 출강, 서울
cyoonj0407@naver.com,
@cyoonj0407

Education
2022 Ph.D. Hongik University, Seoul Korea | 2010 M.F.A. Hongik University, Seoul Korea | 2001 B.F.A. Hongik University, Seoul Korea
Solo Exhibitions
2021 The Breath Pouch, Craft on the hill Gallery, Seoul Korea | 2020 Breath, The Sculpture of Volume, Gallery Ahwon, Seoul Korea | 2019 Craft Trend Fair-Breath, The Sculpture of Volume, COEX, Seoul Korea | 2013 Figure+structure, 57th Gallery, Seoul Korea and 3 times
Group Exhibitions
2023 Decorative Digitalism II, Temple Contemporary, Philadelphia USA | 2023 Cheongju Craft Biennale, Culture Factory, Cheongju Korea | 2022 Ars Longa, Gallery

SP, Seoul Korea | 2021 Craft Trend Fair, COEX, Seoul Korea
Collections·Awards·Activities
SeMoCA, Seoul | 2020 Selected, Arte y Joya Int. Award, Spain | 2020 Honorable Mention, New Taipei City Int. Metal Craft Competition, Taiwan | 2019 Judge's Choice, ITAMI Int. Craft Competition, Japan
Present
Jewelry Artist, Adjunct Professor at Hanyang University, Ansan Korea, Lecturer at Hongik University, Seoul Korea
cyoonj0407@naver.com,
@cyoonj0407

최혜영 Hyeyoung Choi (1985–)
       →72

학력
2021 국민대학교 대학원 졸업, 서울 | 2009 국민대학교 졸업, 서울
단체전
2023 표면의 정서, 갤러리 바움, 파주 | 2022 해후, KCDF 갤러리, 서울
소장·수상·주요활동
포르츠하임 장신구박물관, 독일 | 2021 마쩨 졸업작품상, 갤러리 마쩨, 네덜란드 | 2020 입선, BKV-Prize, 독일 | 2019 입선, 이타미 국제공예공모전, 일본
현재
장신구 작가
chycome@naver.com,
@hye0hye

Education
2021 M.F.A. Kookmin University, Seoul Korea | 2009 B.F.A. Kookmin University, Seoul Korea
Group Exhibitions
2023 Texture External Sentiment, Gallery Baum, Paju Korea | 2022 Reunion, KCDF Gallery, Seoul Korea
Collections·Awards·Activities
Schmuckmuseum Pforzheim, Germany | 2021 Marzee Graduate Prize, Galerie Marzee, Netherlands | 2020 Selected, BKV-Prize, Germany | 2019 Selected, ITAMI Int. Craft Competition, Japan
Present
Jewelry Artist
chycome@naver.com,
@hye0hye

한은석 Eunseok Han (1973–) →55

학력
2002 동덕여자대학교 대학원 졸업 | 1996 동덕여자대학교 졸업, 서울
개인전
2024 우연한 발견, KCDF 갤러리, 서울 | 2020 Stay Alive, 경인미술관, 서울 | 2001 PLAYING, 인사 갤러리, 서울
단체전
2024 Wearing Red, 파티나 갤러리, 미국 샌타페이 | 2024 MASSART Auction, 매스아트 디자인앤미디어센터, 미국 보스턴 | 2023 KURIOS, Neue Residenz Bamberg, 독일 밤베르그 | 2023 Material Revolution, 미국 시카고 | 2023 Tides are changing, 캐나다 빅토리아 | 2023 Contemporania, 팔라우 데 페드랄베스, 스페인 바르셀로나 | 2022 Cluster 주얼리박람회, 영국 런던
소장·수상·주요활동
2023 입선, Arte y Joya 국제주얼리공모전, 스페인 | 2021 우승, JOYA 바르셀로나 아트주얼리&오브젝트, 스페인 | 2023 수록, Ateliers d'Art de France, 프랑스 | 2023 수록, 현대공예의 새로운 미덕, 코리아나, 한국 | 2022 수록, Breaking the mold, 뉴욕타임즈, 미국
현재
장신구 작가
sozoh2@gmail.com,
@eunseok.han.in.seoul

Education
2002 M.F.A. Dongduk Women's University, Seoul, Korea | 1996 B.F.A. Dongduk Women's University, Seoul, Korea
Solo Exhibitions
2024 Serendipity, KCDF Gallery, Seoul Korea | 2020 Stay Alive, Kyung-in Art Museum, Seoul, Korea | 2001 PLAYING, Insa Gallery, Seoul Korea
Group Exhibitions
2024 Wearing Red, Patina Gallery, Santa Fe USA | 2024 MASSART Auction, MASSART Design & Media center, Boston USA | 2023 KURIOS, Neue Residenz, Bamberg Germany | 2023 Material Revolution, Pistachios Gallery, Chicago USA | 2023 Tides are changing, Victoria Int. Marina, Victoria

Canada | 2023 Contemporania, Palau de Pedralbes, Barcelona Spain | 2022 Cluster Jewelry Fair, Koppel Project, London UK
Collections·Awards·Activities
2023 Selected, Arte y Joya Int. Awards, Spain | 2021 Winner, JOYA Barcelona Art Jewellery&Objects, Spain | 2023 Featured, Ateliers d'Art de France, France | 2023 Featured, Finding better ways with craft, KOREANA, Korea | 2022 Featured, Breaking the mold, The New York Times, USA
Present
Jewelry Artist
sozoh2@gmail.com,
@eunseok.han.in.seoul

한은지 Eunji Han (1990–) →70

학력
2019 국민대학교 대학원 졸업, 서울 | 2016 국민대학교 졸업, 서울
개인전
2020 공예트렌드페어, 코엑스, 서울 | 2019 공예트렌드페어, 코엑스, 서울
단체전
2022 일품단장, 서울공예박물관 크래프트 윈도우, 서울 | 2021 Review Reful, 아트비트, 서울 | 2021 15/25, 갤러리 오, 서울 | 2021 블루 불확실한 봄, 갤러리 바움, 파주 | 2021 BKV-Prize, 국제수공예박람회, 독일 뮌헨 | 2020 몸에 그리는 그림, 갤러리 바움, 파주
소장·수상·주요활동
2021 특선, BKV-Prize, 독일 | 2020 입선, 탈렌테, 독일 | 2019 마쩨 졸업작품상, 갤러리 마쩨, 네덜란드
현재
장신구 작가
eunji_1012@naver.com,
@haneunji_artjewellery

Education
2019 M.F.A. Kookmin University, Seoul Korea | 2016 B.F.A. Kookmin University, Seoul Korea
Solo Exhibitions
2020 Craft Trend Fair, COEX, Seoul Korea | 2019 Craft Trend Fair, COEX, Seoul Korea
Group Exhibitions
2022 一品丹粧, SeMoCA, Seoul Korea | 2021 Review Reful, Gallery Artbit, Seoul Korea | 2021 15/25, Gallery O, Seoul Korea | 2021 Blue An Uncertain Spring, Gallery Baum, Paju Korea | 2021 BKV-Prize, IHM,

Munich Germany | 2020 Drawing on the body, Gallery Baum, Paju Korea
Collections·Awards·Activities
2021 Belobigung, BKV-Prize, Germany | 2020 Selected, TALENTE, Germany | 2019 Marzee Graduate Prize, Galerie Marzee, Netherlands
Present
Jewelry Artist
eunji_1012@naver.com,
@haneunji_artjewellery

한주희 Joohee Han (1986–) →24

학력
2020 뮌헨 조형예술대학 졸업, 독일 뮌헨 | 2013 국민대학교 대학원 졸업, 서울 | 2010 국민대학교 졸업, 서울
개인전
2022 DENSITY, 갤러리 주얼러스 베어크, 미국 워싱턴D.C. | 2020 타원, 아틀리에 우르술라 썬클러, 독일 뮌헨
단체전
2024 장식 너머 발언, 서울공예박물관, 서울 | 2023 Dis_Cover, 예올, 서울 | 2023 가로지르다, 갤러리 마쩨, 네덜란드 네이메헌 | 2022/2019 슈묵, 국제수공예박람회, 독일 뮌헨
소장·수상·주요활동
푸른문화재단, 서울 | 달라스 미술관, 미국 | 코미넬리 재단, 이탈리아 | 2023 입선, MANUFACTUM Staatspreis, 독일 | 2020 1등상, Oberbayerischer Förderpreis, 독일
현재
장신구 작가
jooheehan0309@gmail.com,
www.jooheehan.com,
@joo.hee.han

Education
2020 Dpl. Akademie der Bildenden Künste, Munich Germany | 2013 M.F.A. Kookmin University, Seoul Korea | 2010 B.F.A. Kookmin University, Seoul Korea
Solo Exhibitions
2022 DENSITY, Jewelers Werk Galerie, Washington D.C. USA | 2020 OVAL, Atelier Ursula Sunkler, Munich Germany
Group Exhibitions
2024 Beyond Adornment, SeMoCA, Seoul Korea | 2023 Dis_Cover, YÉOL, Seoul Korea

| 2023 TRAVERSE, Galerie Marzee, Nijmegen Netherlands | 2022/2019 SCHMUCK, IHM, Munich Germany
Collections · Awards · Activities
Pureun Cultural Foundation, Korea | Dallas Museum of Art, USA | Cominelli Foundation, Italy | 2023 Selected, MANUFACTUM Staatspreis, Germany | 2020 1st Prize, Oberbayrischer Förderpreis, Germany
Present
Jewelry Artist
jooheehan0309@gmail.com, www.jooheehan.com, @joo.hee.han

현성환 Seong-hwan Hyun (1992–)
→121

학력
2022 국민대학교 대학원 졸업, 서울 | 2019 국민대학교 졸업, 서울
개인전
2023 시간과 흔적, 노드, 서울
단체전
2024 (UN)Avowable Secrets, 알리아주 갤러리, 독일 뮌헨 | 2024 디자인아트페어, 예술의전당 한가람미술관, 서울 | 2024 크래프트 서울, 코엑스, 서울 | 2023 ASIA MON AMOUR, NYC Fringe, 미국 뉴욕 | 2023 물색, 주예소 스페이스, 서울 | 2023 표면의 정서, 갤러리 바움, 파주
소장·수상·주요활동
2023 입선, 탈렌테, 독일 | 2023 전시기획, 물색, 서울 | 2023 전시기획, 표면의 정서, 파주
현재
장신구 작가, 스튜디오 8 대표, 동서울대학교 출강, 성남
hh7319@naver.com
@hhwwan.art

Education
2022 M.F.A. Kookmin University, Seoul Korea | 2019 B.F.A. Kookmin University, Seoul Korea
Solo Exhibitions
2023 Time and Trace, Knowd station, Seoul Korea
Group Exhibitions
2024 (UN)Avowable Secrets, Alliages Gallary, Munich Germany | 2024 Design Art Fair, SAC, Seoul Korea | 2024 CRAFT SEOUL, COEX, Seoul Korea | 2023 ASIA MON AMOUR, NYC Fringe, NYC USA | 2023 Color

of water, Juyeso Space, Seoul Korea | 2023 Texture External Sentiment, Gallery Baum, Paju Korea
Collections · Awards · Activities
2023 Selected, TALENTE, Germany | 2023 Curated, Color of Water, Korea | 2023 Curated, Texture External Sentiment, Korea
Present
Jewelry Artist, Director of studio 8, Lecturer at Dongseoul University, Seongnam Korea
hh7319@naver.com
@hhwwan.art

홍예인 Yein Hong (1995–)
→126

학력
2023 국민대학교 대학원 졸업, 서울 | 2020 중앙대학교 졸업, 서울
개인전
2024 공예트렌드페어, 코엑스, 서울
단체전
2024 기호공감, 갤러리 인사아트, 서울 | 2024 Be Artful, 노들 갤러리, 서울 | 2024 Magnetism, 갤러리 아르쥬엘, 서울 | 2024 디자인아트페어, 예술의전당 한가람미술관, 서울 | 2024 아트마켓, 갤러리 71, 서울 | 2024 크래프트 서울, 코엑스, 서울 | 2023 크래프토이 파크, 갤러리 아원, 서울 | 2023 디자인아트페어, 예술의전당 한가람미술관, 서울
현재
장신구 작가
yeinhong0417@gmail.com, @yein_craft

Education
2023 M.F.A. Kookmin University, Seoul Korea | 2020 B.F.A. Chungang University, Seoul Korea
Solo Exhibitions
2024 Craft Trend Fair, COEX, Seoul Korea
Group Exhibitions
2024 Empathy with Sense, Gallery Insaart, Seoul Korea | 2024 Be Artful, Nodeul Gallery, Seoul Korea | 2024 Magnetism, Gallery Artjewel, Seoul Korea | 2024 Design Art Fair, SAC, Seoul Korea | 2024 Art Market, Gallery 71, Seoul Korea | 2024 CRAFT SEOUL, COEX, Seoul Korea | 2023 Craftoy Park, Gallery Ahwon, Seoul Korea | 2023 Design Art Fair, SAC, Seoul Korea

Present
Jewelry Artist
yeinhong0417@gmail.com, @yein_craft

박송이 Songyee Park

박송이는 라사라RASARA 패션디자인학교에서 패션디자인과 전통 복식을 전공했다. 졸업 이후 2019년부터 한국 문화를 기반으로 「고목komok」이라는 K 컨템포러리 브랜드를 운영해오고 있으며, 1950–1960년대 '사라지기 전 마지막 자의적으로 개발되고 있던 한복'에서 영감을 받아 서민의 삶에 녹아든 실용적인 의복에 대한 작업을 진행해 오고 있다. 2024년부터는 「가지gazi」라는 세컨드 레이블 브랜드를 런칭하였으며, 한국 작가들과 협업 및 전시를 진행해 오고 있다.

Songyee Park studied fashion design and Korean traditional costumes at RASARA Fashion Design School. Since 2019, she has been running her first K-contemporary brand, *komok*, which draws inspiration from the 'final stages of traditional hanbok development in the 1950s and 1960s, reflecting Korean culture. Songyee creates practical and sensible garments that resonate with the lives of everyday people. In 2024, she launched a second label, *gazi*, and has been collaborating with Korean artists to organize exhibitions.

의상협찬 Costume sponsored by

마고자 Magoza top (black)
silk 80%, wool 20%

저고리 위에 덧입는 덧옷인 마고자 정통 한복 패턴을 차용하여 긴 U자 목의 라인이 디자인 선이며 한복 특유의 곡선과 직선의 조화를 잘 나타나고자 했다. 옷깃이 달리지 않고 섶이 덮이지 않아 마주 대어지며, 옆트임이 있고 소매길이는 손목 정도의 길이이며 배래는 직선이 특징이다.

The design is inspired by the traditional Hanbok pattern of the Magoja, worn over the Jeogori, and features a long U-neck that beautifully highlights the harmony of curves and straight lines typical of Hanbok. The collarless front overlaps without a lapel and includes a side slit, while the sleeves extend to the wrist with a straight hemline.

댕기 스카프 DaengGi Scarf
silk 100%

직접 핸드 드로잉 한 고목 시그니처 나이테 패턴으로 구성된 나이테 스카프이다. 자연스러운 톤온톤 배색으로 제작된 나이테의 형상은 자연물의 특성상 각기 다른 패턴을 지니고 있다. 베이직한 아이템에 레이어드 포인트를 더할 수 있으며, 목에 두르거나 머리에 댕기처럼 활용하거나, 허리에 매는 등 다양한 용도로 사용할 수 있다.

The DaengGi scarf features a hand-drawn signature pattern inspired by the growth rings of a tree. Crafted with a natural tone-on-tone color scheme, each growth ring design showcases unique patterns that reflect the characteristics of natural materials. It adds a stylish layering point to basic items and can be worn in various ways–wrapped around the neck, styled in the hair like a DaengGi, or tied around the waist.

100개의 브로치

한국 현대장신구의 새로운 세대

이동춘
국민대학교 조형대학 금속공예학과 교수

2020년 전시 「100개의 브로치－한국 현대장신구 연대기」를 통하여 한국
현대장신구 시대적 변화의 일면을 소개했다. 본격적인 전문 장신구 작가의 출현을
2000년대 초반으로 본다면, 한국의 현대장신구는 짧은 시간, 빠르게 발전하여
국제적인 경쟁력을 갖추었다. 「한국 현대장신구 연대기」 전시는 세대별로
규정하기보다는 활동 시기를 바탕으로 시작Beginning, 전문화Specialization,
확장Expansion으로 분류하여 전시를 구성했으며, 1980년대 초 금속공예를
겸하며, 현대장신구를 대중에게 소개했던 작가들을 포함한 당시 35세 이상의
작가 50인이 각 2점의 브로치를 출품했다.
브로치는 장신구 중에서 상대적으로 표현이 자유롭고, 특히 가슴에 달아 자신의
의도를 매우 적극적으로 드러낼 수 있는 대표적 아이템으로 장식과 함께 다분히
정치적이며 사회적인 사물이기도 하다.

2024년 「100개의 브로치－한국 현대장신구의 새로운 세대」 전시를 이어서
기획하면서 한국 현대장신구의 현재를 조명하고, 이를 통해 미래에 대한 기대를
가늠해 보고자 한다. 이번 전시는 20대 작가부터 40대 작가들까지 50명의 작가가
역시 각 2점의 브로치를 출품, 총 100점의 브로치로 이루어졌다.

한국의 현대장신구는 양적 · 질적으로 빠르게 성장하고 있지만, 그 구조적 토대가
견고하지 못하다. 국내의 이러한 불균형적 환경 속에서도 한국 현대장신구는
이제 새로운 도약의 순간에 서 있다. 그 중심에 있는 젊은 작가들의 고군분투를
응원하며, 현대장신구를 문화적으로 더욱 많은 대중이 향유 할 수 있기를 바란다.

이동춘은 장신구 작가로서 14회 국내외 개인전과 다수의 단체전을 통해 작품을 발표했다. 현재 국민대학교에 재직
중이며, 2000년 현대장신구 전시 「장신구제안」 공동 기획을 시작으로 「플라스틱 플라스틱 플라스틱」(2002,
2017), 「나무-연장된 삶」(2016), 「욕망하는 꽃」(2014), 「100개의 브로치-한국 현대장신구 연대기」(2020)
등을 포함한 전시를 17회 기획하였다. 독립된 장르로서 현대장신구의 개념적 확대와 재료적 다양성을 소재로
전시를 기획하고 있다. 한국 현대장신구 작가 및 전시 아카이브인 www.k-artjewelry.com를 운영하고 있으며,
www.instagram.com/k_artjewelry를 통해 정보를 공유하고 있다.

100 Brooches

A New Generation of Korean Contemporary Jewelry

Dongchun Lee

Professor, Dept. of Metalwork & Jewelry,

College of Design, Kookmin University

In 2020, the exhibition 「100 Brooches–Korean Contemporary Jewelry Chronicle」 introduced the changing face of Korean contemporary jewelry. Considering that the real emergence of professional jewelry artists began in the early 2000s, Korean contemporary jewelry developed rapidly in a short period of time and became internationally competitive. The exhibition, 「Korean Contemporary Jewelry Chronicle」, was organized according to the period of activity rather than by generation, categorized into Beginning, Specialization, and Expansion, and included 50 artists over the age of 35, including those who introduced contemporary jewelry to the public in the early 1980s while also practicing metalwork, each exhibiting two brooches. Brooches are one of the most expressive pieces of jewelry, especially those worn on the chest, they are a representative item that can actively reveal one's intentions, and they are political and social objects as well as decorations.

In 2024, the exhibition 「100 Brooches–A New Generation of Korean Contemporary Jewelry」 was organized to shed light on the current state of Korean contemporary jewelry and to gauge expectations for the future. The exhibition consisted of 50 artists, ranging in age from 20s to 40s, who submitted two brooches each, for a total of 100 brooches.

Korean contemporary jewelry is growing rapidly in both quantity and quality, but it lacks a solid structural foundation. Despite this unbalanced environment, Korean contemporary jewelry is now on the cusp of a new leap forward. By supporting the hard work and commitment of the young jewelry artists at the center of it all, I hope to make contemporary jewelry more culturally accessible to a wider audience.

Dongchun Lee, a jewelry artist, presented his work through 14 solo exhibitions in Korea and abroad, and is currently teaching at Kookmin University. He co-curated an exhibition 「Suggestion」 in 2000 and has curated 17 exhibitions since then, including 「Plastic Plastic Plastic" (2002, 2007), 「Wood-Extended Life」 (2016), 「Flower of Desire」(2014), and 「100 Brooch–Korean Contemporary Jewelry Chronicle」 (2020). Lee has been curating exhibitions that explore the conceptual expansion and material diversity in contemporary jewelry as an independent genre. He currently runs **www.k-artjewelry.com**, an archive of Korean contemporary jewelry artists and exhibitions, and shares information through **www.instagram.com/k_artjewelry**.

한국 현대장신구의 새로운 세대
100개의 브로치

2024. 10. 24 – 11. 03
예술공간 수애뇨339
서울시 종로구 평창길 339 (우)03003

전시기획
이동춘

편집
이동춘

서문/자문
전용일 | 국민대학교 조형대학 금속공예학과 명예교수

기고
브루스 멧칼프 | 장신구작가/저술가
구혜원 | 미술수집가/사업가

번역
박선주 | 번역가 (한글/영어)
백인백색의 만화경―브로치로 본 한국의 현대장신구

이예지 | 장신구작가 (영어/한글)
복합적 형식

이승열 | 국민대학교 조형대학 금속공예학과 조교수 (한글/영어)
이혜진 | 씨앗갤러리 대표 (한글/영어)
덕후(The Koo)의 세계―현대예술장신구 컬렉터 성장기

전시지원/자료정리
이승열, 서예슬, 현성환, 임제운

의상협찬
박송이

도록 디자인
스튜디오 폼투필

후원

A New Generation of Korean Contemporary Jewelry
100 BROOCHES

2024. 10. 24 – 11. 03
Space of Art Sueño339
339 Pyeongchang-gil Jongno-gu Seoul 03003 Korea

Exhibition Planning/Curating
Dongchun Lee

Editor
Dongchun Lee

Introduction/Advisory
Yong-il Jeon | Emeritus Professor at Kookmin University

Articles contributed by
Bruce Metcalf | Jeweler/Occasional Writer
Haewon Koo | Collector/Businesswoman

Translated by
Sonju Park | Translator (ko/en)
A Kaleidoscope of 100 Distinctive Artists―Exploring Korean
Contemporary Jewelry through Brooches

Ye-jee Lee | Jeweler (en/ko)
A Complex Form

Sungyeoul Lee | Assistant Professor, Kookmin University (ko/en)
Jeannie Haijin Lee | Gallerist of Siat Gallery (ko/en)
The World of The Koo―The Evolution of a Contemporary Art
Jewelry Collector

Assistance
Sungyeoul Lee, Yeseul Seo, Seong-hwan Hyun, Jewoon Lim

Costume sponsored by
Songyee Park

Book Design
Studio FORM TO FILL

Patronage
Space of Art Sueño339
Seoul Metropolitan Government
Seoul Foundation for Arts and Culture

사진 Photo By

오정훈 Junghoon Oh
P 20, 58, 128, 136
박광춘 Kwangchoon Park
P 22, 26, 42, 44, 46, 48, 53, 55, 60, 64, 66,
92, 98, 100, 103, 105, 110, 114, 116, 126, 134, 142
미레이 타케우치 Mirei Takeuchi
P 24
이만홍 Manhong Lee
P 28
전병철 Byungcheol Jeon
P 31, 68, 70, 72, 90, 96, 123, 132, 138
박주단 Judan Bak
P 33
김도연 Doyeon Kim
P 38
박용진 Yongjin Park
P 40, 108
백종휘 Jonghwi Baek
P 62
최용석 Yongsuk Choi
P 94
김예슬 Yeseul Kim
P 121
송재희 Jaehui Song
P 140

작가촬영 By Artist

모델 Model